Simon Somerville Laurie

Lectures on Language and Linguistic Method in the School

Second Edition

Simon Somerville Laurie

Lectures on Language and Linguistic Method in the School
Second Edition

ISBN/EAN: 9783337085438

Printed in Europe, USA, Canada, Australia, Japan

Cover: Foto ©Paul-Georg Meister /pixelio.de

More available books at **www.hansebooks.com**

LECTURES

ON

LANGUAGE AND LINGUISTIC METHOD

IN THE SCHOOL

*DELIVERED IN THE UNIVERSITY OF CAMBRIDGE
EASTER TERM, 1889*

BY

S. S. LAURIE, A.M. Edin., LL.D. St. And.

PROFESSOR OF THE INSTITUTES AND HISTORY OF EDUCATION
IN THE UNIVERSITY OF EDINBURGH

SECOND EDITION, REVISED

EDINBURGH:
JAMES THIN, PUBLISHER TO THE UNIVERSITY.
LONDON: SIMPKIN, MARSHALL & CO.
1893

[*All rights reserved.*]

PREFATORY NOTE.

THESE Lectures were delivered at the request of the Teachers' Training Syndicate of the University of Cambridge, and re-delivered at the College of Preceptors, London. The form of Lectures leads to the use of the first personal pronoun more frequently than is desirable. The reader will pardon this.

S. S. L.

UNIVERSITY OF EDINBURGH,
    May, 1890.

SECOND EDITION.

The book has been revised, and a short chapter on the teaching of French has been added. The Lectures have occasionally been broken up so as to make the volume more suitable as a text-book, and certain expressions omitted or modified which are apt to suggest themselves to a Lecturer as effective. Many, however, are left which could not have been excised without altering the whole form of the book.

S. S. L.

UNIVERSITY OF EDINBURGH,
    June, 1893.

CONTENTS.

LECTURE I.

LANGUAGE THE SUPREME INSTRUMENT IN EDUCATION.

PAGE

Education is through the experiences of life. The most potent of experiences is the distinctive national life in all its forms. Function of the school to focus these national influences. There is, however, a universal as well as a national element present in the education of a human being. Excellence of the individual. Formal discipline of Reason would seem sufficient for this. This too abstract to be available in the education of the young. A concrete subject must be found which contains the abstract in its primary form, and at the same time gives substance of instruction. This subject also must be universal in its character if it is to be effective for its end in the fullest sense. That subject is Language—(1) As a formal discipline. (2) As a concrete or real study. (3) As an æsthetic or Art study. By Language is meant primarily the Vernacular, ... 1–19

LECTURE II.

THE REAL AND FORMAL IN LANGUAGE.

Distinction between discipline and training. The comprehension of Language trains as well as feeds the mind, . . 20–27

LECTURE III.

LANGUAGE AS A REAL STUDY CONVEYING SUBSTANCE OF THOUGHT.

(a) Infant stage of Language-teaching. (b) Primary and Upper-primary school stage. (c) Secondary school stage, . 28–42

LECTURE IV.

LANGUAGE AS A REAL STUDY—*continued.*

1. Word-building, synonyms and ambiguities. 2. History of Words. 3. Sentences and Paragraphs. 4. Paraphrasing. 5. Reading and Elocution, ... 43–54

LECTURE V.

LANGUAGE AS A REAL STUDY—*continued.*

1. Oral Composition. 2. Transcription. 3. Elementary written Composition. 4. Abridgments and Narrations. 5. Translations. 6. Imitation. 7. Original Essays or Theses and Reproduction, ... 55–62

LECTURE VI.

LANGUAGE AS A FORMAL STUDY. GRAMMAR.

Method in general. Relation of abstract study to Discipline as distinguished from Training. Grammar a system of Abstractions. Method. 1. *The When:* should not be begun till the twelfth year. 2. *The How Much.* 3. The Method must be the *Real* Method, . . . 63–75

LECTURE VII.

GRAMMAR OF THE VERNACULAR TONGUE. METHOD.

First stage: successive Steps. Second stage: successive steps. Psychological process in parsing. Historical Grammar and Comparative Philology, . . . 76–95

LECTURE VIII.

LANGUAGE AS LITERATURE.

Relation of literature to moral, æsthetic, and religious training. Must be begun early. Method: little to be said of a formal kind. Literary impressions: literary criticism. Importance of Literature in the education of the young. Can literature be taught? 96-123

LECTURE IX.

FOREIGN TONGUES. LATIN AS TYPE.

(a) Reasons for teaching Latin. (b) Method of procedure generally, ... 124-135

LECTURE X.

METHOD OF TEACHING LATIN.

Application of Rules of Method to teaching Latin. Greek, . 136-165

LECTURE XI.

METHOD OF TEACHING MODERN LANGUAGES.

Method as applied to the teaching of French, . . 166-177

SUPPLEMENT.

LANGUAGE v. SCIENCE IN THE SCHOOL, . . . 179-197

LECTURES ON LANGUAGE
AND LINGUISTIC METHOD IN THE SCHOOL.

LECTURE I.

LANGUAGE THE SUPREME INSTRUMENT OF EDUCATION.

Education must be first of all national. There is also an universal element. Through Language we best secure both aims. The educational relations of Language as a concrete subject, a formal subject, and an æsthetic subject.

EVERY human being is educated by the experiences of life. The experiences begin very early. The babe at its mother's breast is receiving impressions for good or for evil as certainly as a seed, which has just begun to sprout, is already absorbing from the soil what is to make it or mar it as a vigorous plant of its kind. Thereafter, as the child walks *non æquis passibus* at his mother's side, the whole world of nature is seeking to form him. Earth and sky, the events of his little life, the words and acts, nay even the gestures, of those about him are all busy in the work of his education. Unconsciously at first, and thereafter consciously, he is organising into himself the vast and infinite material of outer impression and inner feeling.

Every human being undergoes this process of education; and it is not at all a question whether he is to be educated or not, but simply how and to what end he is to be educated.

Neither the unconscious education of environment, nor the conscious education of the school, however, is independent of native predisposition and inheritance. No two human beings are precisely alike in respect of their native capacity to receive experiences and to utilise them for the building up of their characters. There is much, very much,—a much that is almost incalculable, in the instincts and aptitudes of race. It is impossible to compare the Chinese child, the Persian, the Hindu, the Hellenic, the Roman, the British, as we find them in history, and not be convinced of this. Next to the instincts and aptitudes of individuals and of race in determining our education, is the spirit of the race as shown in its national religion, laws, and customs, in its more or less conscious aims as a political society, in its public life and its corporate acts, past and contemporary, and, above all, in the literary expression of its way of looking at the world. These alone, without the help of schools, will, under favourable conditions, make a people, and a great people; and, whatever may be done of set purpose by schools and teachers, national life in its various forms will always be, as it ought always to be, the dominant factor in the education of the young.

It is through the family that these educative influences are best conveyed; and no State is in a healthy condition where the family life is not always the most potent, as it is the nearest, of educative influences. As the pressure of life grows heavier, and social conditions grow more complex, it becomes necessary to appoint a substitute for the parent, but not on this account to supersede the domestic by the public school. The school fulfils its purpose when it is a mere auxiliary of the family. What now is the function of the school in view of these facts?

I have said that it is the individual experiences, and the national life in all its forms as the most potent of those experiences, that chiefly educate; and from this I will draw the conclusion that where schools are instituted, their main function is to focus, so to speak, the life of the nation, and bring its best elements—its language, laws, religion, ethics, art, literature, history —to bear on the young whom we gather into our public seminaries. This we do, in the hope that by so doing we may make sure that the experiences which educate shall not be arbitrary and uncertain, but assured, and wisely ordered to the making of a good citizen. To this end, it is the best in the life of the nation to which they belong that we have to give to the young. All other languages, literatures, histories, are to be regarded as merely contributory to the native elements and the continuation of national character in its highest and best form.

It is always character, indeed, and the highest type of national character, that we as educators have to keep before us, not knowledge. It is an educational truism, that however various a man's knowledge may be, if it does not enter into the texture of his mind, it may as well be on his bookshelves. Knowledge, which is not woven into life and conduct, is so far from being wisdom, that it is often an enemy of wisdom and an obstructor of wise counsel.

But there is an universal element as well as a national element in education, by means of which the best national type can be created. As islanders, we, more than other nations, have this forced upon us. Even setting aside all questions of ideal manhood, we yet must grant that to form the good citizen here and now, we must first form the good man. So thought the ancient Athenian; so thought the Roman, whether he spoke through the mouth of Cato, or Cicero, or Quintilian; so assuredly *must* think the Christian, for he has to seek *first* the Kingdom of God. Hence it is that, when the education of the young is not wholly left to casual influences and custom, we are compelled to ask the questions, What is a good man? and, How shall we form him? The answer to these questions is contained in the science and art of education. Surely, then, this is a subject worth considering by all, necessary to be considered by those who mean to devote their lives to the task of educating.

Both the universal and the national elements in education are passed on to the young, chiefly by Language. Language is intensely national; it is a reflex of the inner mental habit of a people. It is also through their languages, much more than through a knowledge of their institutions, that we share the lives of those nations which have a literature, and absorb those elements of life in which we are ourselves defective. This gives rise to self-criticism, and contributes to the growth of the universal in mind and character, as opposed to the national, the parochial, and the individual. I am not to be understood as suggesting that a child should be educated as a cosmopolitan. The weakening of national individualism enfeebles the personality of each citizen, breaks the springs of action, and dries up the sources of living energy.

Of the education of man in the universal sense, we may say with the Greeks that our aim is ἀρετή, the excellence of the individual after his kind, and that the action of mind in attaining to this excellence is σωφροσύνη, if we give it the sense of self-regulation. This self-regulation, which is the wise conduct of life, is dependent on the Will, which, as the dominant characteristic of man, sets in motion (speaking broadly and sinking metaphysical subtleties) his intelligence and selects his motives. But this intelligence and this will cannot work in the air: materials on which they may exercise their formal activity must be provided, and it is these which the instincts of our nature and the experiences of life furnish to all. The school interposes merely to formulate, enrich, and elevate these experiences, and to focus the principles and aims of life out of which the fabric of motives may be built. A richly endowed mind, however, may be weak in intelligence and will. It is the **power** of discriminating and of rightly reasoning, of separating the right from the wrong, the true from the false, the good from the bad, the wise from the unwise, and of giving effect to our judgments, which must always be the governing aim of education.

Now, if this be so, it may plausibly be maintained that, by exercising the intelligence purely as such—as a system of abstract powers, we shall best fit it for coping with the complex materials of experience; that, by disciplining the mental processes which enter into all knowledge and make it possible, we shall best fit a human being to discern the true, and to regulate his life in accordance therewith. And why so? Because these processes of mind are universal and not partial in their application: they cover the whole field of possible human knowledge and activity. But we cannot do this; because the exercise of the abstract faculties of man is not possible at all in their purity. They can be exercised only in and through material of some sort. That material, no doubt, may be the mind itself in its formal activities; but this kind of abstract exercise is not practicable till the period of adolescence, when the great mass of the population has already escaped from scholastic control. Not the formal and abstract, then, by itself (*i.e.* logic and metaphysics), but the formal as entering into and constituting some *real* subject, something which has substance in it, must be the instrument of intellectual *discipline* with a view to power: and, of all subjects, *that* will necessarily be the most effective which is most universal.

1. The concrete subject which is best suited for training the abstract and formal powers of mind is Language. Here you have mind, in all its formal relations, expressed in a substantial form,—as something not purely abstract, but concrete, and capable of being grasped and handled. By the analysis of language, then, you introduce the young intellect to the unconscious analysis of its own thinking in its whole range. While engaged in this exercise, the abstract powers are so involved in a concrete that is familiar to all, that the formal discipline is not made obtrusive and distasteful. A boy who is intelligently analysing language is analysing the processes of thought, and is a logician without knowing it. And this is the reason why the study of language in its formal aspects has always been regarded as the best preparation for the logician and philosopher, and, according to Quintilian, of the orator also. Hence, too, it is the best preparation for the study of all or any of the sciences.

The formal study of language is the study of the abstract; and as abstraction is difficult to the young (and to the old, too, for that matter), it demands an effort such as the "real" or concrete never does, and hence it is that it gives *power*. A very young child, for example, may receive and enjoy the sentiments of Tennyson's "May Queen," or Wordsworth's "We are Seven," and yet find the formal analysis of the language to present insuperable difficulties: but it is precisely this formal and abstract exercise in the mere vehicle of expression that we must give, if we are to give *power* to the mind.

That the discipline yielded by the study of the formal or grammatical in language gives to the mind power and discrimination to find its intellectual way amid the conflicting experiences and contradictory motives· of daily life, all must admit; but few recognise the close connection between this kind of discipline and moral discipline. Moral discipline is the habituating of the will—the dominant fact and function in a human being—to overcome the difficulties of temptation to stray from what is seen and affirmed to be the right path. But it is the *same will* which I call upon for energizing activity when I present the mind of a boy with the intellectual difficulties of formal studies, and call upon him to overcome these. There are not two wills in a man. The effort, then, which all formal studies demand of the young, that they may overcome intellectual difficulties, is not merely intellectual, but moral, in its effects on character. It is an old saying that labour produces ingenuous minds; and if we translate ingenuous as well-bred, or well-conditioned, we see the truth of the apophthegm.

It may be said with a show of truth, that to attain this great result—intellectual and moral discipline—the language of elementary mathematics, physics, or biology would serve. It would serve, unquestionably, but not so well, because the language of these studies is partial and restricted, whereas the language of which we are speaking—the language of everyday intercourse and of literature—is universal in its sweep, and presents a variety, a delicacy, and subtlety of the thinking process which all the sciences of nature taken together cannot for a moment approach. The language, then, of ordinary human intercourse and of literature is, when pursued as an abstract study—*i.e.* in its historical forms and logical relations—the best of all possible disciplines of the intellect; first, because it is the study of the intellect itself, but this in a concrete material which brings it within the capacity of the immature mind of boyhood; and, secondly, because of its universal character—because, that is to say, all the processes of mind are presented for analysis, and this in every possible relation of simplicity, complexity, and subtlety.

2. This brings us to the second ground of the claim which language makes for a supreme place in the education of youth. Language presents to us not merely the process of *thinking* made visible, the clothed form of thinking, but it is also itself concrete *thought* on all that concerns the life of man as an individual, and as a member of society. There is no aspect of human life, no complication of human motive, no ethical relation, no æsthetic emotion, no religious aspiration, which language, as medium of intercourse,

and as literature, does not convey, and, while conveying, illumine.

Accordingly, important as is the formal discipline which the analysis of logical processes gives as these are embodied in language, still more important are the training and instruction which language, as embodying the substance of thought, yields. It is in and through language that man enters on the inheritance which the past has bequeathed to him. Every word, almost, has a lesson for him. *Verba ante res* is as sound an axiom as *res ante verba*. A large proportion of words introduce the pupil for the first time to moral and religious truths; others define his social relations; others, again, contain in their bosom the counsels of perfection. Nay, there are words which bring into his consciousness not merely one thought, but a whole system of thought. If we wish to train a boy in the true, or the good, or the beautiful, how are we to do it? There is no way but by introducing him to the utterances of the wise and good on those questions, so vital to all, and a right answer to which alone makes humanity worth preserving. Through the perusal of literature alone can man enter into the possession of the hard-won victories of the past, and make himself the fellow and companion of the greatest and noblest of his race —the prophets of all time. The content of literature in its various forms is a moral content, a religious content, and an æsthetic content. It is the substance of mind and the whole of Man.

The substance of thought, it cannot be doubted, is

of more importance in education than discipline in the logical forms by which that substance has been elaborated and expressed. After what has been already said, I shall not be accused of underrating the discipline which the formal or grammatical study of language gives; but yet there can be no doubt that it has been allowed to obscure the education that lies in the *real* study of it. The necessity of acquiring the ancient tongues has led to the exaggerated importance assigned in school—especially in the secondary school—to the pursuit of the formal, *i.e.* grammar, to the exclusion of the substance of the language, the real as opposed to the formal. Far more effectual in moving and raising the mind than any logical analysis of language can possibly be, is the food, the nutrition of thought, which language as literature conveys. What was the Renaissance in its influence on the School, but the substitution of substance for form—the reading of authors instead of grammars, and rhetorics and logics ? \Through substance (it was felt) you may best reach form and the formal itself; through the formal you can rarely, and only by accident, reach substance.\ The Renaissance movement, by identifying itself with form in the sense of style, died of its own elegances.

Let me apply this same conception to the moral and religious sphere. It is to be presumed that in educating a boy you wish to make him familiar with great thoughts, and to inspire him with a high ethical spirit. If you do not aim at this, then in what sense and for what end do you educate at all? Now, it is easy, if only you set about it in the right way, to engage the heart of a child, up to the age of eleven or twelve, on the side of kindliness, generosity, self-sacrifice, and to fill him, if not with ideals of greatness and goodness, at least with the feelings or emotions which enter into these ideals. You thus lay a basis in feeling and emotion on which may be built a truly manly character at a later period. Without such a basis you can accomplish nothing ethical, now or at any future time. But when the recipient stage is past, and boys begin to assert themselves, they have a tendency to resist, if not to resent, professedly moral and religious teaching: and this chiefly, because it then comes to them or is presented to them in the shape of abstract precept and authoritative dogma. Now, the growing mind of youth is keen after realities, and has no native antagonism to realities merely because they happen to be moral or religious realities. It is the abstract, preceptive, and barren form, and the presumptuous manner in which these are presented, that they detest. How, then, at this critical age to present the most vital of all the elements of education, is a supremely important problem. It is my conviction that you can only do so through literature; and the New Testament itself might well be read simply as literature. The words, the phrases, the ideals, which literature offers so lavishly, unconsciously stir the mind to lofty motives and the true perception of the meaning of life. We must not, of course, commit the fatal blunder of making a didactic lesson out of what is read. We take care that it is understood and illustrated, and then leave it to have its own effect. In short, just as language treated on its *formal or abstract* side introduces a boy to logic without his knowing that it does so, so language on its *real* side introduces him to the ethical life in all its relations without his being aware that it is doing so. He gradually forms his own saws out of many instances.

|I will now conclude that language, as formal, is the most effective and universal of all pure *disciplines* possible in the school; and that language, again, as real, is the most effective and universal of all *instructors* of the mind of man.[1] |

3. But this is not all: for language is also the most universal teacher of Art. I shall not venture even to attempt to answer the vexed question, What is Art? But this much, in the interests of my argument, I may safely say. /Art is the beautiful in a concrete form./ What, again, is the beautiful? When we say a thing is beautiful we use a word of complex meaning; no other *one* word can define it. But this at least is a prominent factor in the notion which the

---

[1] "As all civilisation really takes its rise in human intercourse, so the most efficient instrument of education appears to be the study which most bears on that intercourse, the study of human speech. Nothing appears to develop and discipline the *whole man* so much as the study which assists the learner to understand the thoughts, to enter into the feelings, and to appreciate the moral judgments of others."—*Middle Schools Report*, 1867 (vol. i. 4).

word conveys—the beautiful is a feeling of the perfection of a thing after its kind, the ideal of its kind.

In the earlier portion of this discourse, I said that we might very well take the Greek ἀρετή, excellence (or perfection) of a thing after its kind, as summing up in a single word our aim in the educating of a human being, and our own aim consequently in educating ourselves. No man, in whom the process of thinking has been once started, but has an ideal of life for himself more or less consciously expressed. Whether this ideal is truly the ἀρετή, or excellence of Man, it is for the thinkers of the world to say. By the help of these thinkers every nation and every age forms its ideal—the ἀρετή for it; and it is to this ideal that we seek, more or less consciously, to train our children. We cannot say that a man is educated until he is possessed by a *conscious* ideal of life. And this means that a man is not educated until the ordinary precepts and maxims of the understanding, which regulate his conduct, have been conceived by him, not as mere judgments of wisdom, but as *ideas*. Now, to conceive an ordinary maxim of virtue or any form of goodness, as not merely a judicial maxim, but as an idea, is to conceive it as at once instinct with emotion, and as the Divine law of our being. A certain infiniteness and majesty are thereby given to the prosaic and finite maxim; and the idea—be it of benevolence, or of integrity, or of purity, or justice, or holiness, or fortitude, now stands out in our consciousness as at once imperative motive and ideal end of all our doing. It is only now that a man is a spiritual being as opposed to a merely moral being. If, then, we can train so as to give a conscious ideal of life, and so as to raise maxim and precept to the potency of Divine ideas, we have attained our chief ethical purpose as educators: the discipline of life must do the rest.

The study of Art (whatever else it may be) is the study of the idea in the concrete, and the emotion which the perception of the concrete idea evokes is an emotion similar in kind to that which those spiritual ideas that bear on the conduct of life evoke in us. It is not to be supposed that we can moralise a man by art, or that there is salvation in æsthetics. But this may be said, that however immoral a man may be, yet if he is alive to the beautiful in nature and art, he must be, though perhaps an animal, yet a more refined, a more delicate, and altogether a more human animal, than he would be without æsthetic perceptions. The transition from the æsthetic and becoming to the ethical ought not to be difficult. The unquestionably close alliance between the beautiful and the good was fully recognised by the Greeks. All æsthetic training, accordingly, if not put forward as itself moral and spiritual training, but kept in its due place, is to be recognised as ancillary to the spiritual life; and it may even awaken the spiritual in boys and men who are inaccessible to the less sensuous forms of ideas.

Now, the most universal form of Art is to be found in language as literature. Painting has its limits, sculpture has its limits, architecture has its limits. Literature is the universal medium for the expression of the whole range of man's nature under the impulse of the emotion of the beautiful. Its highest form is poetry. But it is also true that, wherever we find apt and felicitous expression of mind, whether in prose or poetry, we have so far a work of art to be admired for its beauty. And this, I take it, means that the expression of thought so conveyed not only engages the activity and the assent of our reason, but touches also our emotions—the emotion of the beautiful, the eternal joy in the ideal.

Thus, and so far, the teaching of literature is a training in ideals; and whether it moralises or not *directly*, it is, certainly, a potent indirect force in the formation of spiritual ideals. Let me give an illustration. The brutality, egoism, snobbery of the English schoolboy is part of history—see the records of fagging, etc., and his peculiar measure of men and things when you meet him. Now, what I venture to say is this, that even were there no moral or Christian education at all from day to day (and it would almost seem that there is little *consciously* aimed at in our public schools, except by an individual here and there), yet, a boy who had been enjoying, in his master's company and that of his schoolfellows, a fine creation of Wordsworth or Tennyson, could not possibly leave the room and go and do a mean or unworthy thing; or if he did, he could not do it without bringing down on his head the reprobation of his fellows and his own self-condemnation. And this, not because of the substance of the thought alone, but because of its form, because of the ideal impulse which it gave—the capacity for "the Idea" which it touched in him. *Honestorum turpiumque nullum est consortium*, says Quintilian; and again Plato in the *Republic* says, "The words of truth and beauty are the best garrison of souls whom God loves," and that because the truth is beautifully expressed. Thus it is that the poets are our great educators: "Through the sweet bait of their numbers they steal into young spirits a desire of honour and virtue." [1]

The beautiful in art or language is not only universal in its character, but it is universal in its relations to the human mind as compared with other forms of art. The material used—language—is familiar to all; all can be made, at least, to understand it; and the great majority may be led by a skilful master to *feel* it, and so be æsthetically trained, by being brought under the influence of art-forms, of the beautiful in the concrete—of ideals.

Enough has now been said to show that, whether we regard the discipline of intellect, the substance of morality and wisdom, or the growth of the distinctively spiritual life (the life in ideas and ideals), language as a formal or logical study, as a real study, and as a literary or art study, is, and must always be, the supreme subject in the education of a human

[1] Edmund Spenser in his *View of the Present State of Ireland.*

being, the centre round which all other educational agencies ought to range themselves in due subordination.

In conclusion, when I say that language is the supreme subject in all education, I mean the vernacular language, with some foreign tongue as a necessary auxiliary. It is not, however, my intention here to advocate English as a subject of school instruction, although I am well aware that Ben Jonson, Mulcaster, and Brinsley have been crying aloud almost in vain for three centuries. I must here assume that the good example set by some schools is universal. But this one argument let me press on the recalcitrant. Mind grows only in so far as it finds expression for itself; it cannot find it through a foreign tongue. It is round the language learned at the mother's knee that the whole life of feeling, emotion, thought, gathers. If it were possible for a child or boy to live in two languages at once equally well, so much the worse for him. His intellectual and spiritual growth would not thereby be doubled, but halved. Unity of mind and of character would have great difficulty in asserting itself in such circumstances. Language, remember, is at best only symbolic of a world of consciousness, and almost every word is rich in unexpressed associations of experience which give it its full value for the life of mind. Subtleties, and delicacies, and refinements of feeling and perception are, at best, only suggested by the words we use. The major part lies deep in our conscious or half-conscious life, and is the source of the tone and colour of language, and of its wide-reaching unexpressed relations. Words, accordingly, must be steeped in life to be living; and as we have not two lives, but only one, so we can have only one language.

To the mother-tongue, then, all other languages we acquire are merely subsidiary; and not to speak here of the introduction these languages give us to other literatures, their chief value in the education of youth is that they help to bring into relief for us the character of our own language as a logical medium of thinking, or help us to understand it as thought, or to feel it as literary art. It is the same with the educative influence of the lives of other nations, such as the Greeks and Romans: these are not to be substitutes for our own national life, nor yet are they to be simply annexed as alien possessions: they do their best work by deepening, broadening, and raising the specific national life. If they do not do this, they are better left alone.

LECTURE II.

THE REAL AND FORMAL IN LANGUAGE.

Distinction between Training and Discipline. The comprehension of a proposition trains as well as feeds the mind. Language, accordingly, as a Real study claims a supreme place in the school.

IN my first Lecture I have pointed out the threefold claim of language to a supreme place in education: first, as a formal or abstract study, that is to say, as a logical and historical analysis; secondly, as a real study, conveying the substance of thought; and thirdly, as literature, in which are presented to us the forms of the ideal—Art.

These three aspects of language will now be looked at more closely. First, I shall treat of language as a Real study, as conveying the substance of thought; but before doing so I shall in this lecture speak of the formal and the real, and of training and discipline in general.

I have said that formal study disciplines the intelligence more than the study of the real. Why, now, does the study of the formal specially discipline? For two reasons: first, because the spontaneous effort demanded of the pupil is greater and more self-sustained than in other kinds of work; secondly, because the formal is only another name for the abstract; and as the abstract is removed to a certain distance (so to speak) from the substance or matter from which it is abstracted, it follows that dealing with the abstract is a purer exercise of the intellectual processes, simply as such, than occupation with the concrete or real possibly can be. Exercise in the abstract thus tends to give greater force to our intellectual processes—a force which, inasmuch as these processes are always the same, is of universal application. An exercise in the abstract approaches in its character the exercise of mind on the formal operations of mind as such. For example, in mathematics, instruction in practical mensuration doubtless both trains and disciplines the mind; but the abstract study of geometry, just because it is formal or abstract, demands more self-initiated and self-sustained effort, and, as a purer exercise of intellect, disciplines the mind more effectually.

The formal study of language I shall henceforth, for shortness, call by the traditionary name grammar. It stands, as we have seen, midway between language as a real subject, conveying substance of thought, and logic. It is logic in its concrete form, and it is language in its abstract form. As such it disciplines in the sense which I have above explained. But while this is so, there is no essential difference between discipline and training. The same processes of mind are exercised in both, but under different conditions. Discipline is a severer kind of training; training is an easier kind of discipline. A great many minds refuse to respond to discipline, but all minds can be trained. There is no essential difference, as I have said, between discipline and training, though there is a distinction; and the point I wish to make is this, that much more can be accomplished for the education of intellect by training than the advocates of discipline have been in the habit of recognising. The question is an important one in its general educational relations as well as in its linguistic; for teachers have too hastily assumed that in the mere understanding of what is read or taught, there is no training of the processes of mind, but only the storing up of information. Let us look at this more closely.

Language studied as the substance of thought is *food* for the mind; but it is so only in so far as it is comprehended. Now, this act of comprehension carries the intelligence through a mental process. This process is necessarily the grammatical and logical process in the concrete, for language is the reflex, not merely of thought, but of the thinking process. But there are various stages of comprehension, rising from the vague and indefinite feeling that something or other has been said, to the partial and fragmentary understanding of what has been said (and this stage again has many degrees), and thereafter, to the final grasping of the thought in all its particularity and fulness. When a piece of language is so grasped that the thought it conveys is reduced, in the mind of the reader, to that order and relative subordination of parts which it had when it first took complete shape in words, his mind has been carried through the mental processes which originally produced the thought and its word-vestment. Now, to the extent to which any mind is carried through such processes of thinking, it is being *trained* as well as fed. This is training: let us now restate by way of contrast the nature of discipline.

It is only in so far as we look at the *relations* of the word-vestment apart from the concrete substance that we deal with the formal in thought and language—the abstract—the logical and grammatical. It is this occupation of the mind with form which, as I have tried to show, gives *discipline* to the intelligence as distinct from *training* (though it necessarily also comprehends training). The fixing of the mind on the formal or abstract, on thinking deprived of the support of the concrete, is a difficult exercise of mind, and rightly not attempted till boys have left school. It is formal logic. The fixing of mind on the generalised character of words and their inter-relations in a sentence is also a difficult exercise; but this, which is grammar and grammatical analysis, is not beyond the reach of the schoolboy, because his mind is supported by the symbols which we call words, and these are presented to his senses. It is by such exercises that we give what is to be distinctively called discipline.

We thus strengthen reason for all particular exercises of whatsoever kind. For the subject-matter of formal exercises is not necessarily this or that *particular* thought or reasoned statement, but thinking, and reasoning, and the conditions of rational expression through words, simply as such. Formal exercises are thus universal in their relations, and extend the range of mental power simply as power, and, while extending, also intensify, the power.

The distinction between training and discipline is, it is to be hoped, made clear. Training has constantly been assumed to be identical with discipline. It certainly is contained in discipline; but I would further point out that it *also* lies outside it, and that training is possible when there is no discipline in the strict sense. This is apparent from what I have said. To the neglect of the distinction between these two educational notions is due the corresponding neglect of a whole side of education. Had schoolmasters been convinced that mental training can be given by the study of language as the concrete embodiment of thought, and that accordingly you could give food to the mind, while, *at the same time*, securing the *training* of it, school would have been a pleasanter place for boys, and the results of school work, both intellectual and moral, would have been much more satisfactory than they have been.

For it is manifest that when a schoolmaster realises that he can truly *train* the mind by getting it merely to understand literature, he will be more ready to believe in the real or substance of language as educative than if he regards reading as giving merely information. He will then see that it is not necessary that the organism of words which constitute sentences should be studied with his pupils formally and abstractly as an organism in order to secure training. It is enough that they be studied for what they convey. And in this there will be a great gain for his pupils. For not only is the assimilation of food a training of the intelligence-processes, but it is food; not only is it food, but it is a training of the intelligence-processes. Now, food is what the hungry want, drink is what the thirsty want, and all human beings hunger and thirst more or less, and so can be trained through their intellectual appetites.

The most real of all "things" are the thoughts of man. One true thought, take it whence you will, once fairly rooted in the mind of a boy, will do more for him, whether he is to be a shoemaker or a statesman, than grammar or the calculus or the syllogism will do. So subtle are the secret relations of the material of feeling and the suggestions of experience which are always flowing into our consciousness, that one such rooted thought quickly finds some worthy mate, and is the mother of a whole tribe. Nay, even a partial thought which fails to sustain itself, but dies where it took root, is not wholly lost; it enriches the soil and stimulates future productivity. Mind is not the machinery of thinking only, but it is a complex of substantial thought; and you nourish thought in the young only by thought.

Let us conclude, then, that by the study of language as a concrete study, as substance, as reality, we both feed and train the mind; we enrich the blood of mind, so to speak, and we, at the same time, teach mind its courses.

Accordingly, if we were compelled to choose between the formal or grammatical, and the real or substance of language in educating youth, we should unquestionably prefer the latter, and leave grammar out altogether. For more than two thousand years the formal has in all subjects been too much with us. Definition, precept, dogma can be easily set down in propositions, and prescribed for a boy's learning. The work is memory work. The progress of the pupil thus seems to be something measurable in respect of quantity, and the master's task is easy; whereas, as a matter of fact, the true process of education is a matter of quality, and is not measurable.

You will not conclude from this that I am disposed to depreciate the formal in language—grammar. I have shown its bearing on the discipline and strengthening of the mind in all its relations, including the conduct of life. But it is quite consistent with this to hold that in the education of a boy or girl, language is to be regarded mainly as a concrete study, and that, as the medium of all experience and of all thought, it claims a much more dominant place in the school than has hitherto been assigned to it, on this ground among others—that it *trains.*

What is the actual state of things? The technical arts of reading and spelling being acquired with more or less success, the teacher's work is thereafter largely restricted by himself to the formal or grammatical. You certainly discipline the mind in this way, but, most assuredly, you cannot so best educate it. The growth of mind and the growth of language in the mind go together. There has to be organised in the boy the language of his inner life, so that the language may grow with the life and the life may grow with the language. Now, this great object can only be attained by the pupil's reading and re-reading, and comprehending the thoughts of others as expressed in fitting words, and by his expressing his own observations and thoughts — native or borrowed — in fitting words. Both these intellectual occupations must be carried on together.

LECTURE III.

LANGUAGE AS A REAL STUDY CONVEYING SUBSTANCE OF THOUGHT.

Method of acquiring Language. **Infant stage.** *Primary school stage. Secondary and advanced stage.*

LET us now consider Method with reference to the study of Language as substance of thought. Our aim here is not to teach reading and writing, but to put the young in possession of language as the articulation of thought.

I shall be here very practical, and take the different stages of language-teaching as these are fairly enough indicated by the external division of school-work—the Infant stage (to the age of seven), the Lower and Upper Primary, and the Secondary.

(a) *Infant* Stage *of Language-Teaching in relation to Thought.*

In the child up to the eighth year, the range of language is very small; he probably confines himself to the use of not more than two or three hundred words. Our business as educators is to give to these words definite and clear significations, and to help the child in adding to his stock. For in adding to his stock of understood words, we add to his stock of understood things, and, consequently, to his material for thought and the growth of the fabric of mind.

In doing this we must follow the method which nature is itself pursuing : the pupil is daily and almost unconsciously adding to his store, in conversing with others and in hearing the names of the common objects which pass daily and hourly before his eyes. The infant teacher, then, will not only respect—taking care that they are clarified, so to speak, and used in a determinate sense—the store of vocables already acquired, but will add to the stock in seven ways, and so promote the parallel mental growth.

1. By conversing with the class on any subject suggested by the incidents of the day or of the classroom, in such language as, while it may be in advance slightly of that which the children themselves use, is yet within their comprehension if they make a slight effort. Teachers seem to forget that children have ears through which they at *this stage* can acquire more than from a printed book.

2. By telling them simple stories, and narrating or reading to them fairy tales. Some educationalists have objected to fairy stories for children because of their fictitious character. It suffices here merely to point out that the imagination of little children is very active in the sphere of the possible and impossible ; that this

normal activity of the imagination contributes largely to the growth, culture, and enrichment of mind; and that it has to be taken advantage of by the educator who respects law wherever he finds it. Where would Homer and Sophocles have been had they not imbibed mythological lore with their mother's milk? Even the genius of Shakespeare would have perished in the thirsty desert of a childhood of bare facts. I would further say, in passing, that what applies to children, applies *à fortiori* to the adult; and that fiction, the drama, and art, ought, in consistency, to be excluded from all life by those who would deny the unreal to children. It might also be shown, were this the place to do so, that in the active imaginations of children and their appreciation of fairy stories, we see at work, in a rudimentary way, the capacity for the ideals of art and religion. In any case, let children *listen* to readings by the teacher.

3. By means—and this, at the earliest stage, chiefly —of object-lessons. Here words are learnt in close connection with the sensible things they denote.

4. By means of the reading-lessons and examination on them, or rather conversation about them. You will see the importance of the kind of reading-books which should at this early period be preferred. They must contain all the ordinary words of child-life; they ought also to contain a gradual and graduated extension of the child's vocabulary; and give expression and shape to his infant thoughts and growing conceptions of the world and man.

5. By means of verses—*e.g.* nursery rhymes first, and thereafter verses regarding incidents of child-life, and descriptive of simple, moral, and religious story. These should be learnt by heart for repetition and singing.

6. By calling on the children to give an account, in their own words, of lessons they have read, or stories that have been told to them.

7. By means of writing in the later stage. The writing of words, and simple sentences consisting of a few words, does much to lay the foundation of accurate expression—even though such exercises be only transcriptions from a book or blackboard.

(b) *Primary and Upper Primary School Stage.*
(7 *or* 8 *to* 14.)

The above procedure is continued, but in advanced form. The transcription of passages and the recitation of verses are at every stage a part of the second method.

When the pupil has left the infant-stage behind him, that is to say, when he has got his second teeth, and can take a firmer bite of the outer world (so to speak), and his fingers a firmer hold of all that comes within reach of his sense-tentacles, his instruction in language, as the highway to thought, as the gateway of the humanities, is, so far as the school is concerned, generally regulated by the reading-books used. These language lessons constitute for the boy (except among the wealthier classes) his whole literary curriculum. How important it is, then, that they should be so constructed as to fulfil the requirements of a literary course. By means of a good collection of prose and poetry, we extend the range of thought and language. This is not to be done by reading one book devoted to one subject. Accordingly, collections of good pieces are to be preferred, and several books should be read — some with great exactness, others cursively.

The question of method at this stage resolves itself very much into this—How shall we best use the reading-lesson as a lesson in language, and through language in the humanities? Here, more than anywhere else, the cultivation, the knowledge, the sympathy, the imagination, the educative skill of a teacher reveal themselves. The reading-lesson is the common ground on which the true mind of master and pupil meet.

I take it for granted that object-lessons, including nature-lessons, are always going on, and that, by means of these, the words of the pupils are gradually increasing in number and in exactness of application. But this is a small matter compared with the training in language as the vehicle of that which is not given to us through the senses, of that which is the product of the human spirit at work on the things of sense and the facts of human life and conduct.

We must always bear in mind that every pupil has,

as yet, technical difficulties to encounter in reading the lesson prescribed. The lesson is, in fact, not merely a lesson of thought, or feeling, or imagination to him, but also a lesson in the deciphering of words, and in articulate utterance always allow for this.

The lesson (we shall say) is on "Courage," or "Truthfulness," presumably well written as regards form, and illustrated by examples.

To begin with:—What is the subject before me as a subject of instruction and education? Manifestly the lesson as a whole, that is to say, the thought, the moral teaching of the lesson in its totality. And next, what are the units of the lesson on which I must base my detailed examination? Not the individual words, but the sentences.

Accordingly, we should proceed thus:—

1. On giving out the lesson we should tell the subject of it; we should try to bring the children's minds *en rapport* with the subject by conversing with them briefly about it; all in a very informal and easy-going style. This we do in order that we may bring what the pupils *already* know to bear on the fresh thought or information which they are about to receive. Thereby the unknown lesson grows out of the known, and is an organic, and not a mere mechanical, extension of the thought of the pupil. "This, now," we say, "is what the lesson you are going to prepare speaks about, and you have now to go and make out the sentences, and find what the writer has

to say on the subject, and we shall read it together afterwards."

2. We then see whether there are in the lesson any words wholly new, and to these we direct the attention of the class by means of the blackboard, and give their meanings; and this can be given only in connection with words already known.

The pupils are then expected to prepare the lesson for the following day.

A purely *narrative* lesson is easily disposed of. We do not need in such a case to follow pedantically the above mode of procedure, unless there be some special point, moral or other, which the writer, or we, desire to bring into prominence. To this we should cursorily allude, and that would suffice; but we ought not to speak of it in such a way as to deprive the lesson of its novelty or its surprises.

3. On the following day the lesson is read with due regard to the rules of reading, and the master then proceeds to examine on the *general* scope and import of the lesson *as a whole*. What is it all about? What does it mean to tell us or to teach us? This is the totality of the reality before him, just as, *e.g.*, the *whole* apple is the totality of the object in an object-lesson on the apple. This process the teacher goes through with the books (including, above all, his own book) shut.

The idea (pray, mark!) at the bottom of the examination on the lesson as a whole is, that it is a quiet and rational conversation between an instructed mind and less instructed minds, with a view to extend knowledge on **the** basis of knowledge already possessed. And this idea must run through all examinations on the *whole* **of a** lesson, from the infant school **up to** the age of seventeen. When this is lost sight of, the art of examination is lost. Think of a man doing this sort of thing with a cane in his hand or with severe magisterial airs!

4. **The next** step is to take the units of language (which **I have said** are the sentences) in their order *with the book open*; just as in an object-lesson I give **the** total object **to perception first, and** thereafter proceed to look at the units which make up the total object,—which units are qualities,—so now I take the sentences of **the** lesson as parts of the whole. Each sentence is read again, and, after being read, the master asks such questions as will bring into view its various parts and relations, as well as the significance of the individual words. This is the preliminary stage of what, as **an** abstract study, we know as analysis, *i.e.* it is an analysis in relation to **the** synthetic or concrete, which must always precede the **abstract** and formal, if the latter is to be intelligent, *i.e.* have a *real* basis.

5. The lesson should now again be viewed *as a whole*, having a beginning, a middle, **and an** end; and **the** children should be asked to give an account of it in their own words. One **or** two **of the** more fluent attempting this, the rest will be too happy to lie in wait for omissions and errors, with a view **to** supply and correct them. In this way, the lesson, whether it be descriptive, narrative, or didactic, will be reproduced

by the combined efforts of the class. The master will then read the lesson to the pupils himself, as it ought to be read, they having their books shut. Thus, the ear is trained.

6. The teacher may now also, at this stage (and with the books shut), enter on the familiar and colloquial illustration and extension of the subject of the lesson, in more or less detail, according to the time at his disposal. He will call on the pupils for voluntary contributions to the subject, in the form of facts drawn from their own experience, or for thoughtful suggestions. Thus is the lesson " turned to use " by being made productive of many deductive or collateral lessons. It is at this stage that the practical application of the lesson, if it be a moral one, comes in. Do not dwell too emphatically on this, however, as if children were so constituted that they naturally resented moral and spiritual ideas. Take for granted that they are children of God.

It may not be possible to do all that is suggested above for want of time; but it is none the less necessary to understand what should be aimed at, if we are to do for a complex literary lesson what is done for a complex object of sense, when we give an object-lesson.

So much for the lesson as a whole, and in its individual sentences; but addressing, as I do, those who mean to be teachers, I would go now more into detail with the fourth step in the examination process—that in which we deal with sentences. By so doing I shall make clear what is meant by the teaching of words in relation to thought. It is presumed that the boy is at the end of the primary stage, that is to say, about fourteen years of age.

Take the following passage as illustrating how much training as well as instruction (which, let me repeat, is the *building up* of knowledge in the mind out of the knowledge already there) may be extracted from a few lines, bearing in mind that the questions and answers are merely the skeleton of a prolonged conversation. (The book is, of course, open.)

> "*Every student who enters on a scientific pursuit, especially if at a somewhat advanced period of life, will find not only that he has much to learn, but much also to unlearn. Familiar objects and events are far from presenting themselves to our senses in that aspect, and with those connections, under which science requires them to be viewed, and which constitute their rational explanation.*"

Q. What kind of student is referred to here?
A. The student who enters on a scientific pursuit.
Q. What is said of such a student?
A. That he has much to learn.
Q. Is anything else said of him?
A. That he has much to unlearn.
Q. The author says that every student of a science has much to learn and unlearn; but he says that this is more particularly true of a certain class of students; what class?
A. Those who begin at an advanced period of life.
Q. What is meant by the word "student"?
A. One who studies.
Q. And what do you mean by studying any subject?
A. Reading about it, and thinking about it.
Q. The student referred to is, you have told me, the student "who enters on a scientific pursuit"—pursuit here means subject: What is meant by a *scientific* "pursuit or subject"?

A. A subject carefully arranged, so as to show its facts, causes, and reasons.[1]

Q. **This** explanation is difficult for you **to understand; you will** best explain it by an example.

A. Astronomy, Geology, etc., **are** " scientific subjects " or sciences; that is to say, the real facts about **the stars** (not merely what seem to be the facts at first sight), arranged **so** as to show their connections and causes, constitute the science of the stars, or **Astronomy** (and **so** of Geology).[1]

Q. Can any of you **now,** looking carefully at the sentence, shut the book and give me the **substance of it** in your own words?

A. **A** person beginning to study a science will find that he has much **to learn as** well as to unlearn, and this all the more if he is grown up **before he** begins.

Teacher. We shall **now take the** second **sentence.**

(**The** *teacher here reads* **it** *slowly, while the pupils follow with the eye.*)

Q. What is here said about " familiar objects and events "?

A. That they are " far from presenting themselves," **etc.**

Q. What things are " far from presenting **themselves," etc.?**

A. " Familiar objects and events."

Q. In the science of Astronomy, for example, what would **the** " familiar objects and events " be?

A. The heavenly bodies and their **motions.**

Q. Which are the *objects,* **and** which the *events?*

A. **The** bodies **are** the *objects,* **and their** motions **are the** *events.*

Q. **Now** the author says that these objects and events are " **far from presenting themselves in** a certain **aspect** and connection : " **What do you mean by " aspect "?**

A. Appearance.

Q. What by " connection "?

A. Their union **with each other, or other things,** or their relation to these things.

Q. What kind **of appearance and** connections **do** they fail to present themselves to **our senses in?**

---

[1] **Of course** an answer of this sort is **worked out by the help of the master, and** must be the result of many leading **questions which call to memory all** that a boy already knows in **this department of** knowledge.

A. The appearance and connections under which science requires them to be viewed.

Q. Does the author say anything else about that "appearance" and "connection"?

A. Yes. He says that they constitute their rational explanation.

Q. What "constitutes the rational explanation" of *what?*

A. A certain aspect and certain connections of objects and events constitute the rational explanation of these objects and events.[1]

Q. Can we accurately say that an aspect or appearance and certain connections constitute an explanation of anything?

A. No. What is meant is that the presentation of them to the mind in a certain light, and with certain connections, "constitutes their rational explanation."

Q. What is meant by "constitute their rational explanation"?

A. That the kind of presentation referred to is such an explanation as satisfies the reason of a man.

Q. Now, can any of you, looking carefully at this sentence, shut your book and give me the substance of it in your own words?

A. The author says, that "things to which we are accustomed, are not always seen in such a way as science requires them to be looked at, and that the way of looking which science requires gives us an explanation of these things which satisfies our minds."

Teacher. Now, take your slates and go to your seats. Your composition lesson to-day will be putting these two sentences in your own words. In doing this you may make as many sentences of them as you please.

I select the above sentence from Herschell, because it is representative of the graver kind of prose reading suited to the age of fourteen or fifteen—the transition from the upper-primary to the secondary stage of education.

A school library must furnish the cursive reading, and it should do so abundantly.

[1] *Vid.* note on preceding page.

(c) *Secondary School Stage.*

Of this Secondary stage all that can be said is, that you go on as you have begun, taking care, when perusing an essay or treatise, to exercise the boys in the analysis of its reasoning as a whole, so as to reach the principles on which the argument ultimately rests. With this one remark I might dismiss the subject of Language as a *real* study in the Secondary School, especially as we have more to say under the head of Language as Literature. But before doing so, let me further illustrate my argument by citing passages which may fairly represent the prose reading of boys between fifteen and eighteen :—

OF RECREATION.

"Spill not the morning (the quintessence of the day !) in recreations. For sleep itself is recreation. Add not, therefore, sauce to sauce; and he cannot properly have any title to be refreshed, who was not first faint. Pastime, like wine, is poison in the morning. It is, then, good husbandry to sow the head which hath lain fallow all night with some serious work."—THOMAS FULLER.

CARE OF OUR TIME.

"God hath given every man work enough to do, that there shall be no room for idleness; and yet hath so ordered the world, that there shall be space for devotion. He that hath the fewest businesses of the world, is called upon to spend more time in the dressing of his soul; and he that hath the most affairs, may so order them that they shall be a service of God; whilst at certain periods they are blessed with prayers and actions of religion, and all day long are hallowed by a holy intention. . . . Idleness is the greatest prodigality in the world; it throws away that which is invaluable in respect of its present use, and irreparable when it is past, being to be recovered by no power of art or nature."—JEREMY TAYLOR.

LEARNING AND GENIUS.

"Besides, who can tell whether learning may not even weaken invention in a man that has great advantages from nature and birth; whether the weight and number of so many other men's thoughts and notions may not suppress his own, or hinder the motion and agitation of them, from which all invention arises; as heaping on wood, or too many sticks, extinguishes a little spark that would otherwise have grown up to a noble flame. The strength of mind, as well as of body, grows more from the warmth of exercise than of clothes; nay, too much of this foreign heat rather makes men faint, and their constitutions tender or weaker than they would be without them. Let it come about as it will, if we are dwarfs, we are still so though we stand upon a giant's shoulders; and even so placed, yet we see less than he, if we are naturally shorter sighted, or if we do not look so much about us, or if we are dazzled with the height, which often happens from weakness either of heart or brain."—SIR WILLIAM TEMPLE.

The thinking out of such passages as these alone with boys and girls in a kind of conversational examination will do much to feed and train mind in the largest sense; and if a boy is made to *apply himself* independently to the comprehension of such passages, he will also have his pure intellect so far disciplined. In any case, it must be self-evident that we cannot carry a boy through such readings without giving him intellectual *training*, as well as substance of instruction. He is led to accompany the writer step by step in his thought, and so, without being aware of it, he is being exercised in the processes of thought, by identifying his own thought-activity with that of another and more mature mind. Such intimate fellowship with thinking must make a boy thoughtful. If there is intellectual training to be got anywhere, it is surely to be got here. The study of *Oratio* teaches *Ratio*.

I should like to complete the school study of language as substance of thought, by reading with a youth of seventeen or eighteen the *Advancement of Learning*, Bacon's **Essays**, with the help of Whateley and Abbott, and Locke's *Conduct of the Human Understanding*. In such studies there is true education of the whole mental capacity. There is nutrition, training, and discipline, such as a youth cannot possibly get from painful exercises in extracts from Greek authors. It is at this stage, too, that historical readings from our best writers are introduced, and large and rational views of world history have their beginning.

We often hear of the value of translation from a foreign tongue into our own. The English studies I advocate are translations from the more difficult to the more easy,—translations, moreover, in which the finding of equivalent terms by the help of dictionaries will be of little use without a close study of the thought of the writer.

"A boy reading the vernacular," says M. Fouillée, "is carried along by the general sense of the passage, and is not compelled to attend to details and delicacies of expression as when he translates from a foreign, especially any ancient, tongue." True; but this superficiality is what good method exists to prevent; it secures the benefits which translation gives, and secures the result which M. Fouillée rightly thinks so valuable— the making the work of the thinker and writer his own.

LECTURE IV.

LANGUAGE AS A REAL STUDY CONVEYING SUBSTANCE OF THOUGHT—*continued*.

Method—continued. Word-building. History of Words.

I TRUST it will now be granted to me that in teaching language as a concrete or real subject we truly *train* the mind, although we cannot, perhaps, be said, in any strict sense, to discipline it: Logos means Reason as well as Word. The right method of effecting this training in language with a view to the growth of the individual life and thought, through the comprehending of the thought of others, has also been briefly put before you. The question of method, however, as applied to instruction in the *substance* of language, is far from being exhausted. Numerous subsidiary processes may be thought of by the teacher, and some of these I shall now advert to.

1. *Word-building.*—The great majority of the words in use are not English, but Latin. The compositeness

of the English Language is one of the causes of its value as an educative instrument, as it is of its power of delicate and various expression. Mere custom will, of course, give a knowledge of the signification of these foreign words, especially of those which have become thoroughly domesticated. But even with these, and still more with all the others, a thorough acquaintance can be gained only by a conscious analysis of their elements. The mere statement of the root helps very little. The word "element," for example, has just been used by me; but I get little light as to its signification by being told that its root is *elementum*. Better tell me the meaning in English at once, and then give me *elemental*, *elementary* as derivatives. It is clear that if we are to give boys effectually the derivatives of any simple word, we must introduce them to the prefixes and affixes, and exercise them in the precise force of these. This is far more important, and (like everything that is important in education) far more interesting, than the Latin origin of the word, which in itself, and by itself, is often barren of all intellectual nourishment, except, of course, when it is part of a Latin lesson.

With those words, however, which are fruitful, and have a progeny, the root is most instructive. To confine ourselves to words used here within the compass of a few lines, let us take "signification." It unquestionably is of great value in the acquisition of the language to know the root *signum*, a sign, and, having understood this, to build on this foundation, signal, signify, signification, significant, significance, design, designation, etc., resign, resignation, etc., consign, and so forth. All these words are then bound together by a common root-idea, and are thus better remembered, and ever after more correctly used; and let us never forget that the correct use of a word is the correct perception of a thing. So, "constitution:" here we have *stare*, to stand, and out of it we have a numerous progeny. Can any one doubt the value of this kind of exercise? Is it not, indeed, indispensable, if we are to take possession of our native tongue—the sole vehicle of expressing our own thoughts, and understanding the thoughts of others? Let it be carefully noted that this kind of instruction is not to be given from text-books and in the form of lessons, but must arise casually out of the daily reading, the pupils having note-books in which they enter all that is of value. Interest disappears the moment you leave the page before you and try to give a formal and didactic character to word-teaching, apart from the living use of language. The teaching, moreover, is in that case easily forgotten, because of its being divorced from its natural associations. So much for the architecture of words.

It may be objected that, while prefixes and affixes substantially retain their meanings wherever used, English vocables derived from the Latin, especially when they have come to us not directly, but through the French, frequently lose their primary meaning. But the fact that this is so, or that the primary meaning has acquired connotations in the course of daily use, gives them an additional claim on our attention, and additional importance as a mental training. The words we acquire by scientific study are like the words we acquire through an object-lesson, as meagre as they are simple. White is white, horse is horse, and there is an end of it. But the words which carry down through the ages the thought of man, and not merely his fact-observation, are complex in their nature, subtle in their relations to each other, full of imagination, rich in history. They are the *mind* of man in an objective form—nature itself speaking in all its richness, and not in scientific formulæ; and were we to substitute for them the boasted exactness of scientific terms, we should destroy our inheritance. Mankind would have to begin over again: there would be nothing left but the "prairie value" of our opulent estate.

2. *History of Words.* — These remarks naturally introduce us to our second subsidiary process under the head of method—the *history* of words as distinguished from the formal building up of words. This is a most stimulating study for the young, especially in the secondary school stage. It is itself a kind of historical education, and calls forth and cultivates the imagination in a variety of ways.

The history of words is well handled by Archbishop Trench in his well-known book (whether he is always etymologically accurate or not is beside the present question). The moral and intellectual benefit to be derived from this kind of teaching is too obvious to require more than mention. Take, for example, "idiot," which means originally only, in the language from which it comes, a "private person;" then a man either careless of public duties or incompetent to exercise them; hence a man uneducated and with undeveloped intelligence; finally, an "idiot" in the present sense of the word. Much significant instruction, surely, for the young citizen here.

So also many lessons—lessons full of moral substance—may be drawn by the intelligent teacher from such words as "simple," "silly," "virtue," "honour," and so forth. These and numerous other words illustrate the history that is in all words, save those that record a mere sense-fact. And yet we are told to teach "things," that is to say, realities of sense and not words, because words are barren! Why, it is through words first of all, as *vehicles* of things—things of the mind—that we learn all that is worth learning. Wendell Holmes well says, "By words we share the common consciousness of the race which has shaped itself in these symbols." Again, "Every word we speak is the medal of a dead thought or feeling struck in the die of some human experience."[1] "Words," again says Emerson, "are fossil poetry."

In further enforcing this teaching of word-history, I cannot do better than introduce Archbishop Trench to plead for it. After speaking of "tribulation" as derived primarily from *tero*, to rub, from which came

[1] *Elsie Venner*, chap. xxviii.

tribulum, a threshing-sledge (which was a wooden platform studded with iron teeth underneath), hence *tribulare*, to crush and oppress, he says:

"This word some Latin writer of the Christian Church appropriated for the setting forth of a higher truth; and sorrow, distress, and adversity being the appointed means for the separating in men of whatever in them was light, trivial, and poor from the solid and the true, their chaff from their wheat, he therefore called these sorrows and trials 'tribulations,' threshings, that is, of the inner spiritual man, without which there could be no fitting him for the heavenly garner. Now, in proof of my assertion that a single word is often a concentrated poem, a little grain of pure gold capable of being beaten out into a broad extent of gold-leaf, I will quote, in reference to this very word 'tribulation,' a graceful composition by George Wither, a prolific versifier, and occasionally a poet, of the seventeenth century. You will at once perceive that it is all wrapped up in this word, being from first to last only the explicit unfolding of the image and thought which this word has implicitly given; it is as follows:—

"'Till from the straw the flail the corn doth beat,
Until the chaff be purged from the wheat,
Yea, till the mill the grains in pieces tear,
The richness of the flour will scarce appear.
So, till men's persons great afflictions touch,
If worth be found, their worth is not so much,
Because, like wheat in straw, they have not yet
That value which in threshing they may get
For till the bruising flails of God's corrections
Have threshed out of us our vain affections;
Till those corruptions which do misbecome us
Are by Thy sacred Spirit winnowed from us;
Until from us the straw of worldly treasures,
Till all the dusty chaff of empty pleasures,
Yea, till His flail upon us He doth lay,
To thresh the husk of this our flesh away,
And leave the soul uncovered; nay, yet more
Till God shall make our very spirit poor,
We shall not up to highest wealth aspire;
But then we shall: and that is my desire.'"

"Great will be our gains—our pupil's gain and ours," the Archbishop goes on to say, p. 42, "for teacher and taught will for the most part enrich themselves together—if, having these treasures of wisdom and knowledge lying round about us, so far more precious than mines of Californian gold, we determine that we shall make what portion of them we can our own, that we shall ask the words which we use to give an account of themselves, to say whence they are and whither they tend. Then shall we often rub off the dust and rust from what seemed to us but a common token, which, as such, we had taken and given a thousand times; but which now we shall perceive to be a precious coin bearing the image and superscription of the great King; then shall we often stand in surprise, and in something of shame, while we behold the great spiritual realities which underlie our common speech, the marvellous truths which we have been witnessing *for* in our words; but, it may be, witnessing *against* in our lives. And as you will not find (for so I venture to promise) that this study of words will be a dull one when you undertake it yourselves, as little need you fear that it will prove dull and unattractive when you seek to make your own gains herein gains also of those who may be hereafter committed to your charge. Only try your pupils, and mark the kindling of the eye, the lighting up of the countenance, the revival of the flagging attention, with which the humblest lecture upon words, and upon the words especially which they are daily using, which are familiar to them at their play or at their church, will be welcomed by them. There is a sense of reality about children which makes them rejoice to discover that there is also a reality about words; that they are not merely arbitrary signs, but living powers; ... not innumerable disconnected atoms, but growing out of roots, clustering in families; connecting and interwining themselves with all that men have been thinking and doing and feeling from the beginning of the world till now.

"And it is, of course, our English tongue out of which mainly we should seek to draw some of the hid treasures which it contains, from which we should endeavour to remove the veil which custom and familiarity have thrown over it. We cannot employ ourselves better. There is nothing that will more help than will this to form an English heart in ourselves and in others."

In the more advanced stages, synonyms and ambiguous words should receive attention (see Appendix to Whateley's *Logic*).

3. *Sentences and Paragraphs.*—I have already shown in the examination on a sentence from Herschell how we should proceed in order to secure full comprehension of a passage by the pupil, and to make it the basis for an extension of his linguistic and general knowledge; but I introduce the subject here again for the purpose of saying that, as boys grow in years, much more may be aimed at and accomplished than I have yet suggested. If you wish to see what this "more" is, I refer you to Locke's *Conduct of the Human Understanding*—a book too seldom read by teachers and others. And I shall here hold it as read, and so save space and time.

4. *Paraphrasing.*—To facilitate the full comprehension of difficult sentences and paragraphs, the exercise of paraphrasing came into general use in this country about twenty-five years ago. Paraphrasing consists in the turning into commonplace language, which "any fellow may understand," the verses of a poet, or the succinct prose of such writers as Bacon and Browne. A more detestable exercise I do not know. It is a vile use of pen and ink. One would, of course, submit to it as an unhappy necessity were there no other way of showing that we understand an author. But this is very far from being the

case. To paraphrase Milton or Shakespeare, is to turn the good into the inferior or bad, and to degrade literature. Moreover, it is false. For the youth who has done it imagines that his bald sentences give all that is to be found in the original passage of Milton or Bacon. If this were so, then there would, alas! be no such thing as literature, no such thing as Art in language. When all is done, you have no longer got Bacon or Milton, but only your much lesser self. This exercise is based on a misunderstanding of the whole situation.[1] Teachers were vaguely groping for some means of assuring themselves that their pupils really saw their way through the organism of a piece of poetry—terse, elliptical, and frequently inverted in the *ordo verborum*. But this object can quite well be attained by a process which might be called "Resolution," or, to please those fond of big words, "Dialysis." It simply consists in the writing out of the piece of poetry in grammatical prose order, supplying words understood, but *always preserving the language of the poet*. This prevents a boy from contenting himself with that vague knowledge which is not knowledge at all, but mere impression supported by dim, disconnected images, or, it may be, by the mere musical sounds or rhythm of language. It compels him to be exact, and may, perchance, startle

---

[1] Quintilian may be thought to approve of paraphrasing; but a careful reading of the passage (x. 5) shows that paraphrasing with him was, in truth, rather imitation—certainly not the paraphrasing of our examination halls. Ascham, again, with reference to Latin says, "Paraphrasis is not mete for grammar schools."

him for the first time into the perception that poets, after all, talk plain sense, and may thus awaken his critical faculties. To shut the book and try to express the substance of the thought of a prose writer in your own words is an excellent exercise, but this is not "paraphrasing" as commonly practised.

5. *Reading and Elocution.*—To read well is difficult. It is a rare accomplishment: nowhere more rare than among teachers of elocution.

The secret of good reading lies in the practice (*a*) of *distinct articulation* (even a little exaggerated in the case of very young children), (*b*) of deliberateness, These conditions secure reading that is intelligible. (*c*) Emphasis comes next—the emphasising of words in clauses, so as to bring out their relative importance. (*d*) Further, I would direct the teacher's attention to what I should call Phrasing: that is to say, the regulating of the rapidity and intonation of subordinate clauses so as to bring into view their subordinate character. The necessary prior conditions of all good reading are, of course, the full comprehension of the passage to be read and the opening of the mouth.

All this is quite teachable and attainable in the lower-primary stage, and may be much improved in the upper-primary. But more than this we cannot expect (save where there is a genius for reading), and we ought not to try to get more. If we call upon children to add to intelligibility and emphasis and phrasing, the emotional and imaginative as dramatic elements, we at best secure a wooden imitation of somebody or other—a falsetto elocution. Nothing can be more hurtful or more offensive. The teacher, however, may so read the passage to them as to bring out its full emotional meaning, if he feel himself competent to do so.

In the secondary school stage, we may begin to aim at really good reading. We shall finally attain our aim only when there is a combination of physiological, intellectual, and emotional conditions, which, though not so rare as the natural qualifications for good singing, is in truth a gift of nature. We may approximate to it in a good many cases, however. To begin with, it is based on imitation, and yet it is not to be got by the mere imitator. There is always a certain originality in it which an elocution master never respects, but which has to be respected if we are not to call forth mere slavish imitation of a model. This makes reading artificial and false. Good reading comes from within. It is not acting,—no, not even when reading a drama. The reader has always to subordinate himself to his author, and let *him* speak. As to the best style of reading, I like much the words of Quintilian: "Reading should be manly and grave, but grave with a certain sweetness." Comenius' rule, "present a good model," is in reading specially applicable. All teachers of English should be good readers, and should read to their pupils much more than they do.

As to the reading of ordinary prose, I think we approach nearest perfection when we read what is in the book as if we were *speaking* our own thoughts. But it is difficult to appropriate from a printed page what another says, and then say it as from oneself. It is, in truth, a complex psychological process.

But all this about reading is intended in the interests of language-teaching. For, by reading well, training in language as the vehicle of thought—as a mental process uttered—is largely aided, not only in the case of the reader, but of those who hear him. Good class-reading is thus one of the most valuable of the imitative processes by which a boy acquires language; while the practice of it also contributes to the growth of æsthetic perceptions.

LECTURE V.

LANGUAGE AS A REAL STUDY CONVEYING SUBSTANCE OF THOUGHT—*continued*.

Method—continued.

Expression of a Pupil's own Thought in Language.

Oral Composition, Transcription, Elementary Written Composition, Abridgments and Narrations, Translation, Imitation, Original Essays, and Reproduction.

THE growth of mind, if it is to be an effectual growth, must be at the same time the growth of language. In many and subtle ways they act and react on each other. This must be so, because language is merely the externalising of the inner life of mind.

1. *Oral Composition.*—In giving rules for language-teaching in the infant school (Lecture III.), I had to include the synthetic exercise of putting words together so as to form sentences, as both an oral and a written exercise; but above all, as an oral exercise at that stage.

It would be superfluous to repeat what was then said; but I must assume that, through the whole period of education, the rules laid down are duly observed. Much may be done to aid oral composition, by always requiring a complete sentence from the pupil in reply to questions. However scurvily we adults may treat our noble language, content to convey our meaning in any sort of way, the process of education assuredly demands that language, simply as language, be respected.

The habit of oral composition should be kept up during the whole school period.

2. *Transcription.*—To make boys and girls sit down and write out, with due attention to legible writing and punctuation, prose paragraphs and poems from celebrated authors, is an admirable exercise. It gives linguistic material. At all ages, but especially in the earlier years of language-teaching, this exercise should be almost a daily one. Why should we dwell on the many advantages that belong to this practice? Is it because it is so simple that teachers disdain it? Much of teaching and much of learning is unnecessarily laborious, because teachers will not do what is simple and natural and obvious. There is no strain in this exercise, and it is all the better for that.

In connection with transcription we naturally mention the learning of good pieces of literature by heart. It is these two exercises, along with much intelligent reading and intelligent conversing on the basis of the day's lesson, that constitute the imitative in language-education; and they are as remarkable for not overstraining the powers of mind as they are for building up these powers in the healthiest possible, because the most natural, way.

3. *Elementary Written Composition.* — The next stage in training to the expression of thought is the formation and writing of connected sentences, either in answer to some question naturally arising out of the reading lesson, or in the record of some incident of the day. Though I am opposed to the early beginning of formal grammar, I think that at a very early age, say eight, the attention of pupils should be directed to the fact that a proposition or sentence is an affirmation regarding something or other, and that the distinctions of "subject" and "predicate" should be taught. *By frequent observation of numerous examples on the blackboard,* and not by definition or the expounding of the teacher, children quickly learn this logical groundwork of the sentence, and their knowledge can then be used to correct the sentences which they themselves are required to write on their slates. In this way they will very soon get a firm and solid hold of the structure of a sentence. In examining the sentences made, the teacher should invite the children to inspect each other's productions; and he should always select some sentence shown up to him which contains a typical blunder, and place it on the blackboard for the criticism of the class. It is well also to select

the sentence or paragraph which he considers the best and write it on the blackboard, and if he can improve on it himself he should do so there and then.

In all such lessons, Composition text-books are to be avoided. They are not only superfluous, but hurtful. Children should learn to express themselves in connection with the ordinary reading-lessons, the lessons in history and geography, and the ordinary events of the day. Exercises should always arise, as a matter of course, out of the day's experience. The moment we formulate processes in a text-book and give the book to the children, the formal, pedantic, and formidable aspect of the subject frightens the pupil, and misleads him into the notion that he is required to do something very hard and uninteresting, whereas he is really engaged in what is natural and pleasant. The elements of composition should be acquired without the children knowing that they are acquiring them.[1]

4. *Abridgment and Narrative Writing.*—The next stage is to accustom the pupils to write *consecutive* paragraphs which contain an abridgment of the day's reading-lesson, or of the lesson in geography or history or which reproduce something read to them. The stories read should, up to the beginning of the upper-primary period, be *Æsop's Fables*, and pieces of this

---

[1] The teacher should have one or two text-books for his own private guidance.

class. This for many obvious reasons which it is unnecessary to give in detail. In order to compel the children to see when they have made a complete sentence, each sentence should be written for a time as a separate paragraph. **Abridgments** should frequently be made with the book open. Abridgment and reproduction take the form of *précis*-writing in the secondary stage; and by *précis*-writing I mean the reproduction of some historical narrative or some report, so arranged as to bring out its leading points logically and clearly and briefly.

5. *Translation.* — During the secondary stage of education, and indeed also in the last year of the upper-primary, advantage should be taken of the study of a foreign language for the purposes of English composition. The day's lesson should be written out in good English. There is, probably, no exercise so useful as this for giving a command of the native tongue. In the first place, the materials are provided, and the pupil has simply to think of the language he shall use: linguistic expression, as such, is thus brought into prominence. In the second place, the language to be used is *suggested*. In the third place, the contrast between the foreign and the vernacular comes into relief and compels attention to the comparison of the two, thereby evoking that consciousness of language which it is one of our aims to give. In the fourth place, the different turns of expression which must be resorted to, when translating into the vernacular, lead

the pupil to *weigh* words and phrases and idioms, and to decide as to the right and wrong, the better and the worse. Thus not only is his range of English extended, but the critical faculty, as applied to language, is cultivated. The imagination, as well as the judgment, is exercised.

6. *Imitation.*—About the close of the secondary stage, it may not be a bad exercise to require youths to read a good deal of an author, such, say, as Addison, or Macaulay, or Burke, and to write on some subject in their style—not at all with a view to acquire that style, but mainly as an exercise. But I cannot attach much importance to imitation, though it had a leading place in the rhetorical schools of the ancients. In the case of a foreign tongue, on the other hand, whether ancient or modern, I am disposed to think that a youth who means to acquire style, in addition to grammar, should select some one good author, and always write in imitation of him.

7. *Original Essays or Theses and Reproductions.*— The word essay is a hateful word: it is associated with so much in schools—especially girls' schools— that is false and hollow and showy. The Romano-Hellenic word Thesis or Theme is perhaps less objectionable. Independent essays on subjects prescribed may be begun as early as the upper-primary period, if you confine the subjects to a narrative of what has been experienced, or to a description of something

which *has been seen*. Abstract subjects, such as Patience, Fortitude, Justice, and so forth, are wholly out of place, and indeed ridiculous, till the age of sixteen or seventeen at the earliest; and, even then, compositions on such subjects should be written confessedly (and not furtively) on the basis of treatises by good writers. They thus become essentially reproductions, and are harmless. They are also useful in so far as they enable boys to try to fly with their own wings, and if they should fall, they fall much to their own advantage, and not, like " Lucifer never to hope again." Letter-writing, giving an imaginary account of a journey, is a useful form of original composition; and I need scarcely add that no boy or girl should leave even a primary school without being taught to use the ordinary forms of business or social correspondence.

But whatever is done, let it arise out of the daily work and occupations, or contemporary events, and be natural and not forced. Matter before form. No one can build without building materials. And always remember that it is chiefly by the extensive and critical reading of good authors that we get possession of our own or any other language. Schoolboys should read much more in school or for school than they do. It is true that we cannot be said to possess language, or anything else, till we can *use* it: but we must first have the language to use; and this we shall never get out of the miserable scraps read in school, even when supplemented by boys' books of adventure.

8. Attend to the rule of Method, *Present a good model.* I have seen **teachers** labour at composition for months with very poor results, simply **because they did not** themselves write on the blackboard or dictate, and require the pupils to copy, **their** own perfected specimen of the exercise which had been called for.

9. The rule as to *exactness* in linguistic work is as applicable to the native tongue as to a foreign. Corrected exercises should be returned, to **be rewritten and shown up a** second time. **Masters may be assured** that this **is the** *quickest* **way of attaining their end.** One exercise thoroughly **revised** and rewritten **teaches** more composition **than a dozen loosely done.**

NOTE 1.—The teacher should have a list in his own possession of the more common errors in composition, and give exercises on these.

NOTE 2.—By instruction in the language of books, in accordance with the suggestions in Lecture IV., the acquisition of the power of accurate composition will be greatly aided.

In these lectures I am speaking of the primary and secondary **periods** of instruction **only.** As to the graces of style : these, I **think,** cannot be taught till the university **stage.** In universities, **rhetoric, free from** the **pedantry of figures** and formulæ, **can be made a** most cultivating **study.**

Let us **now** look at language-instruction in its Formal **or** Abstract character, *i.e.* **as Grammar.**

LECTURE VI.

LANGUAGE AS A FORMAL DISCIPLINE. GRAMMAR.

METHOD IN GENERAL.

I HAVE entirely failed in the preceding argument if it does not now appear to every unprejudiced mind that language taught as a concrete subject, that is to say, with special reference to the substance of thought, both nourishes and trains the mind—nourishes it intellectually and morally, and trains it by carrying it through the processes of thinking, which find their concrete embodiment in the forms of utterance. Our own language, indeed, at once nutrifying and training, must always be the main instrument of education: it is only by an ample and adequate treatment of it that the teaching of the school can be made contributory to the maintenance of the national life, and, above all, to the supreme ethical purpose of man's existence as an individual and as a member of a society. Let the young then read largely with understanding.

But there is such a thing as *Discipline* of intelligence; and this discipline, as distinguished from training, is most directly and effectively insured by formal or abstract studies, such as arithmetic, mathematics, grammar, and logic; and this because the occupation of the mind with the abstract is the nearest approach to the occupation of mind with itself as an organism of thinking. Education without discipline must be held to be defective, both as an intellectual and moral process. Discipline, in brief, is an essential part of all education, intellectual and moral, of a rational being; but it is always to be kept in due subordination to nutrition and training—especially up to the age of puberty.[1]

Given, then, that we recognise the significance of the teaching of the formal in language with a view to the education of a mind, the question now is, How shall we proceed? In other words, What shall be our method?

Now, we cannot adequately deal with method in teaching grammar without applying the principles and rules of Method. Were this the time and place, I should ask you to follow me through an analysis of the movements of the human mind in learning anything whatsoever, with a view to the deduction of these rules from the Science of education. As I am now, however, dealing with the Art of instruction

[1] *Moral* instruction, training, and discipline have to be separately treated. It is only in so far as intellectual training and the study of language bear on them that they enter into our argument in these lectures.

alone, I must assume these rules as established. They are not rules applicable to grammar alone, but to all subjects of instruction. I shall draw on them only so far as necessary. As deduced by me from the Science of education, they will be found briefly summarised in the Appendix.

A few words, in addition to what has been said in past lectures, on the nature of the abstract, will introduce us to our fundamental principle of procedure in dealing with the abstract and formal in education. Man does not live upon abstracts. There is no feeding in them. And yet he is for ever abstracting and generalising, correctly or incorrectly, consciously or unconsciously. He perceives anything only by determining it as a single; but if he stopped there, the world of knowledge would be a world of isolated atoms. He sees the common in the diverse, and then proceeds to abstract and generalise. But this he does, not for the sake of the abstract or general in itself. It is merely a logical device, so to speak, whereby he attains to a true knowledge of the individual real things themselves, as they truly exist in all their complexity. The general and abstract, in short, reveal to him a community of character and principle in the diverse, and so help to reduce all to a unity of fact and process of which all individuals are only the particular manifestations or cases. The moment we begin to play with abstractions, without constant reference to things, we find ourselves in a sea of troubles. Accordingly, abstraction and generalisation, while they start from real things, must return also to real things; they interpret them by showing their relations and common ground.

The occupation of the intelligence with the abstract is, as I have said, in a special degree, a discipline, because in contemplating the abstract we are not far from the contemplation of mind itself in its nakedness as a living process, and are thus making an almost direct acquaintance with the organon of all knowledge. But this is not in the truest and fullest sense education, but only that part of it which we call discipline: it is to be compared to the sharpening of the edge of a tool and the strengthening of the body of it for some practical purpose. Grammar, as the logic of common speech, is a system of abstractions. And, like all other abstractions, it must be always kept in close intimacy with the real, on which it rests—the real of words and sentences, if the abstractions are to have any significance at all for the mind of a boy; or, for that matter, of a man. As to method;

1. The formal or abstract in language—in other words, Grammar—should not be begun until the mind of the pupil is sufficiently advanced to be able to grasp it. "Of course not," will be the general response to this obvious proposition. And yet this rule of method is scarcely ever attended to in practice. My own opinion is (but this is a matter on which there will be difference of view) that the beginning of the twelfth year is quite the earliest age at which grammar can be effectively taught — taught so as to be educative

in its effects. At an earlier age it is hearsay knowledge. Prior to the age of eleven, and indeed very early, a child should, by the help of numerous examples, be taught to recognise the subject and its predication—the *whole* logical subject, that is to say, and the *whole* predicate—as constituting a sentence or proposition. This formal condition of a possible sentence can not only be taught very early, but it is for practical reasons desirable to teach it early.[1] A recognition of this fundamental fact of both grammar and logic is very helpful in enabling children to understand what they read, and to express what they desire to express. Beyond this one grammatical fact we should not go until the pupil has entered his twelfth year. Before this age, grammar has no place, either in the infant school or the lower-primary, that is not usurped.

The first objection which will meet us is this: Inasmuch as a subsequent rule of method demands that foreign grammars should be based on the native grammar, we should, by not beginning native grammar till the twelfth year, have to postpone Latin and French till the thirteenth at the earliest. To which my answer is: By all means; why not? In the case of boys and girls who are intending to study French and Latin, there would be no objection to giving them, by the help of the blackboard, a certain number of French or Latin vocables before the beginning of the thirteenth year — names of the familiar things of

[1] In a previous lecture I have said at eight years of age.

ordinary experience, and making use of these to teach correct pronunciation and a few of the more common phrases of ordinary intercourse. But more than this it is not desirable to do. I am speaking of general school education: the merely imitative acquisition of French or German in the nursery—mere memory work at best—lies outside my present argument. But let me repeat here, in passing, that children should be made to live in the atmosphere of their mother-tongue alone, and think through the vehicle of it alone, if we are to promote in them depth and solidity of nature and unity of character.

2. As the first rule of method concerns the "when," so a second rule of method concerns the "how much." The rule of method to which I refer is that which requires us always to keep the *practical* aim in view. "Turn everything to use which you teach, and teach nothing which you cannot turn to use." This is a large question, and would afford materials for much interesting discussion were I writing a big book on method instead of a brief course of lectures. I must be excused for dealing here somewhat dogmatically with this, as indeed with some other requirements, of method.

You at once see that you would not shovel the whole of grammar, even in the restricted school range of this subject, into the mind of a child in his first year of studying it. And yet we all know that in the department of Latin this was done for hundreds of years, and still is done in many places—not only the whole of the formal generalisations, but the exceptions to boot.

Here we have to encounter the obvious remark which all of us can for ourselves put into the mouth of a certain class of teacher before he utters it: "And yet they got up their grammar somehow, and knew it too, perhaps better than any of your modern boys brought up on your new-fangled methods." To this I reply, "Did *they*? Who were the "they"? The teaching of Great Britain, in its secondary schools, has been, till quite recently, exclusively the teaching of Latin and Greek. A few clever boys out of the thousands who have passed through the schools—boys whose brains were such that they would have mastered Egyptian hieroglyphics and Etruscan inscriptions, with all that has been written about them, if these had been *prescribed*—have, of course, overcome the defects inherent in the no-method of the past through the innate energy of their own minds. But what of the rest? Is it not high time that classical masters should cease to throw dust in the eyes of the public on this subject?

In this connection I would have you observe an irresistible claim of sound method. It is this: it always, and at every point, secures the education of the mind. By this I mean that at whatever point a boy's study of a subject may be arrested, he has yet received from the study, so far as it has gone, *an education in the exercise of the processes of mind* which is not measurable by the quantity of material annexed, but is yet the most potent of all disciplinary influences in his future intellectual life. If method as opposed to no-method does not accomplish this, but merely makes the acquisition of this or that subject quicker and surer, it can have little interest for the philosophical educationalist, though it may still retain its attractions for the practical instructor. But as regards mere acquisition, it is notorious that "no-method" has been a scandalous failure. Let us then give method a chance.

Let us return to the "how much," as determined by practical use. What is the practical use of English grammar as distinguished from pure intellectual discipline, which intellectual discipline may be called a theoretical use? I answer, first, the enabling a boy better to grasp the language of literature; and, secondly, the enabling a boy better to express his own experiences and thoughts (when he has thoughts to express). Do you think you do this by the detailed analysis of sentences now in vogue? Beyond that general analysis which brings into relief the logical construction of a complex sentence, you do not help the boy. You present him with linguistic riddles to solve, and make his native tongue as offensive to him as was Latin when it meant a mass of Latin rules in Latin. Let us protect our vernacular literature, at least, from this barbaric dissection, and not defeat the literary purpose we should always keep prominently before us in teaching language.

We have been speaking of the "how much" we should teach in all, that is to say, up to the close of the secondary school course, the age of seventeen complete, at which point I place the proper termination of the secondary school. But it is evident to you that the "how much" applies equally to each successive year of study, and that we must limit each year of study by the age of the pupil, and by what we can at each successive period turn to use. All else is useless; all else is positively hurtful.

Here now enter the subsidiary rules of method: "Little at a time, and that little well." "Little by little, step by step, step *after* step." "Without haste, but without rest;" and so forth.

It may seem strange to you that one lecturing on method should (especially after what he has said in his first lecture) insist so strongly on the practical, and keep out of view the theoretical aim, the formal discipline of the intelligence. It would be too long a task, and carry me too far into the psychology of method, to explain this. But if I did, you would find the result to be this, that a sound theory or philosophy of instruction and education is always practical, both in its instruments and its aims. Further, that a sound method of mere *instruction* is also a sound method of mental *discipline*; that the one secures the other, and thus the two duties of the teacher—discipline and instruction—are harmonised.

3. *The method of procedure must be* REAL. The

real, the real, and again the real—that is the one governing word, not only in all *matter* of education, but also in educational method, especially in the sphere of the formal and abstract. In teaching real subjects, such as literature, geography, science, it is manifest enough that the method must be real; but what I say is, that in teaching formal or abstract subjects, such as grammar, arithmetic, mathematics, logic, rhetoric, the method must be real—that is to say, the abstract must rest on the concrete, be led up to through the concrete, and return to the concrete. For, in truth, there is no abstract in the universe, and there is no abstract in the mind of man which is not an abstract of, and in, the concrete. Hence the rule of method to which I am directing your attention, viz. the abstract and general, must always be taught through the concrete.

We have spoken above of the abstract in general: this is a fitting place to repeat the substance of what was then said, but now in specific relation to the subject of language. Language, as an abstract or formal school study, is the study of those generalisations of likenesses and differences in vocables, and in the organic relations of these in propositions, which, with the addition of the external history of word-forms, we usually sum up under the one name Grammar. When, again, we generalise the characteristics of continuous composition, its logical sequence and persuasive characteristics—all viewed in relation to the attainment of its end, whatever that end may be, whether to please or convince—we call the body of generalised rules and maxims of composition which the analysis yields, Rhetoric. Grammar and Rhetoric, alike, necessarily tend to become a complicated body of organised rules, and as such to be an object of study with a view to *correct* expression in the one case, and *eloquent* expression in the other. Now, the learning of the body of grammar, even with examples tagged on, will not make a *correct* writer, nor will the learning of the rules of rhetoric, with illustrations tagged on, make an *eloquent* writer. Nay, I go further than this, and hold that neither the one nor the other will even enable you to appreciate grammatical accuracy and nicety on the one hand, or literary form and the secret of oratorical or poetical beauty on the other.

To be of any utility, either as a discipline, or as training, or as knowledge, grammar and rhetoric have to be studied through examples. Grammar has to be studied in and through *sentences*, and to be extracted from sentences by the pupil, if it is to be *really* taught; and so also rhetoric has to be studied in and through the masterpieces of literature, and extracted from them, if it is to be *really* taught. This last sentence, indeed, sums up the true significance of the Revival of the fifteenth and sixteenth centuries in the department of education. The meaning of the Revival was not always fully comprehended by the teachers of the time. Hence the belief in style simply as style, and the craze of the Ciceronians. Hence, too, the inevitable reaction and retrogression in the school to words, rules, and forms, to the neglect of the realities of literature and of observation. Accordingly, the Baconian school, when it arose, was perfectly justified in its assault on "words;" and to this day it is justified.

It is, in truth, in the interest — the perennial interest — of the revival of letters that we call on teachers to note that grammar and rhetoric, if taught as abstract systems, are a mere aggregate of names, dead names. These so-called "arts" must be taught in close connection with the living body of flesh and blood on which they rest. To illustrate this in detail would carry me beyond my present purpose. I am content thus far to have brought before you the distinction between language as a real study, and language as a formal or abstract study, and to have emphasised the further fact, that in teaching the formal we should do so *really*, if we desire to succeed in our educative aim. "Matter before Form," says Comenius.

All this is said in vindication of what I consider to be the leading rule of method in all formal subjects, which is, that they should be taught, much more than they are, as real subjects, and in their practical relations; and that the methods should be real. Grammar, in brief, should always be taught in close relation to the use to which words are put in expressing a thought, and the functions of each word and phrase and clause in the thought as expressed; and, however advanced a pupil may be, the secret of maintaining a living intelligence is always to keep returning to the "real" on which the formal reposes.

4. From what has been said, it follows that grammatical rules are to be taught, not logical rules. Grammar is the logic of speech, but it is not logic. A logical statement of word-relations is the logic of grammar; and as grammar itself is an abstraction, the logic of grammar is the abstraction of an abstraction, and incomprehensible by the young mind.

The above remarks on the teaching of grammar are of general application. Let us now pass to the teaching of the grammar of our native tongue.

LECTURE VII.

GRAMMAR OF THE VERNACULAR TONGUE.

Method.

WHAT I have here to say necessarily involves a repetition of the principles laid down in the previous lecture, but now considered in a specific reference.

It is apparent from the nature of an examination in a sentence of English, with a view to the thorough understanding of it,—an examination which I gave you in a former lecture,—that the pupil who *fully* comprehends it, has already analysed words and clauses in relation to *thought*, and performed an important analytico-synthetic exercise. He may now be said to have an implicit knowledge of the grammar and analysis of the sentence. Our object in teaching grammar is to make the implicit knowledge explicit and conscious, and to do this we classify words and clauses under certain abstract generalisations or heads which we call Noun, Adjective, and so forth, according to the function they respectively discharge in the expression of a thought. We then generalise the logical connection of the words and the rules observed in connecting them, and we call this Syntax.

Grammar, then, is the analysis of words and sentences, with a view to collecting together all those words and clause-relations that are like each other under a common designation or name. The exercise, accordingly, is pre-eminently analytico-synthetic, or inductive.

At the risk of repetition let me say: we are not now teaching concrete realities by means of their symbols—words and sentences; we are teaching the generalised and abstract relations of words and sentences; and our instruction is therefore formal, and no longer concrete. It is Grammar.

When we carry this analysis further, and deal with the inner logical development of any writing, and proceed still further to its æsthetic characteristics, we train (as I have said above) in real logic and rhetoric.

The scope of our grammar teaching is limited by what is practicable within the years of school life, and must therefore be so taught that at *whatever stage a boy's education ceases, he shall have obtained the benefit which grammatical teaching is supposed to give;* in other words, that the purpose of teaching it shall be so far attained.

Now, this purpose is to give discipline by means of a highly analytico-synthetic exercise of an abstract or formal kind, whereby we make him conscious, through the concrete, of intellectual processes; and further, to give greater command over words and their relations, as used by others and by himself.

Method: First Stage.

1. I think that the second rule of method (*see* Appendix), which requires us to adapt subjects of instruction to the growth of mind, demands special attention in our consideration of the way of teaching grammar, or the analysis of language. We must not burden the young with this abstract work too early. By the perusal of simple literature as a synthetic study after the method already laid down, and by the practice of composition as an imitative exercise, a boy is subjected to the *training* which language gives without deliberately dissecting it. My opinion is that we should rely on these exercises almost solely till a boy enters his twelfth year. Prior to this, however, and solely with a view to obviate the blunders that pupils constantly make in imitative composition, it is recommended that the division of every sentence into subject and predicate be given even as early as the ninth year, and constantly applied on the blackboard to correct errors in the sentence-making of the pupil. Nothing more than this, in my opinion, should be taught up to the beginning of the twelfth year, and then the dissection of language should be set about as a daily exercise. In what way?

2. We are dealing with generalisations, consequently we ought not to *give* these general words called the

parts of speech, or rules of syntax, to our pupils, but guide them in the attempt to find them out for themselves. This is what is meant by the *real* method. You do not, however, leave the pupil to flounder unaided: you propound to him the object of search, just as a science professor would propound the object of search to his pupils in a laboratory. For example, the proper analytic exercise consists in seeking for those things among a multitude that have a common character, and collecting these together under that common character, to which you then give a *name*. This is a generalisation. But in teaching the very young we must lead the way by telling them the character which we are seeking; *e.g.* this sentence, "the warm sun shines by day, and the bright moon and twinkling stars by night," having been written on the board, we ask for those words that are names of things. These being picked out and arranged in a column by themselves on the board, we next give a few additional sentences, and proceed in the same way. The words thus brought together as "Name-words" in the column are then revised, and the first lesson in grammar is given. The child has brought them together *himself* with your co-operation and guidance.

Thus we fulfil two rules of sound method, for we teach generalisations as generalisations, *i.e.* through particulars, and we get the pupil to instruct himself.

3. The next step is to pick out name-words from the day's lesson, and to give this as a slate exercise in

school or to be done at home. Thus we fulfil the rules of sound method which require us to repeat and revise, and further to *turn to use*, what has been acquired. We may at this stage substitute the word *noun* for "name-word," but we should, in the whole course of grammatical teaching, be continually testing the pupil in the knowledge of the simple meaning and force of all the technical words used, and this because they are Latin and abstract terms.

The greatest difficulty you will meet with at this stage of teaching will be the recognition by the boy of those nouns which are names of things not sensible. This is because a considerable power of *abstraction* is necessary to the mere identifying of them. You overcome this and other difficulties only by frequent repetition of the same sentences and continual construction of similar ones on the blackboard, taking care to confine yourself to simple, or, at most, compound sentences. Exposition will not be of much use. By constant presentation of instances, the pupil learns to form his own abstract.

Never give a lesson of more than ten minutes' length. Three lessons of ten minutes each daily are of far greater advantage than one of sixty minutes. Thus we fulfil the rule, "Little by little."

4. We now proceed gradually in the same way (*i.e.* step by step, little by little, repeating and revising, and turning to use daily) with *adnouns* (or adjectives), then *for-nouns*, then *verbs*, and then *adverbs*, giving five or six lessons, at least, to each new part of speech.

A verb should be introduced as a "doing or telling word," and an adverb as qualifying a verb. But a mechanical help may be given (in the case of verbs) by suggesting to them to try a word by putting "*I*" before it and see if it makes sense.

5. Having reached this point, we should pause a while until we are satisfied that these generalisations are thoroughly known; in this way obeying the rule demanding *exactness* as necessary if there is to be a sure foundation for the next step, further knowledge being an organic growth out of what is known (assimilation, apperception); obeying, too, the further rule which requires us to dwell long over the *beginnings* of a subject. [If we put "*a*" and "*the*" among the ad-nouns, which is the simplest way of doing, as well as, perhaps, the most correct, we reduce the parts of speech to seven, for interjections do not count; and of these seven, the five most important are now acquired.]

In the course of three or four weeks from the date of beginning, provided there is continual turning to use of the knowledge gained, we may go on to prepositions, and thereafter to conjunctions. When the words under a class-name are limited in number, as in the case of conjunctions and prepositions, I would have the children make a list of them as they occur, and enter them in a grammar note-book, with which each child should be provided. In this way the child gradually makes his own grammar-book, and the rule as to self-instruction is fully operative.

The pupil, before he has begun this grammar course,

is presumed, remember, to be familiar with the things and names "subject" and "predicate." If he is not, you must interpose this instruction before you can rationally teach conjunctions.

6. The next step is to teach number. This we do by asking the children themselves to make the plural, and then putting down such words as they may make —*e.g. horse, horses; church, churches*—on the board. The pupils quickly see that the one word denotes a *single* thing, and the other a *more-than-single* thing; and we may now teach the terms "singular" and "plural," as more convenient. Thus we follow the rule of teaching through the senses, and the further rule of constructing the abstract term out of particulars known.

7. Having become familiar with singular and plural in a single lesson followed by a home exercise, we can now have an amusing exercise in *exceptional* words, such as mouse, ox, sheep, and so forth. Thus you follow the rule, "The prominent or salient facts of a subject should be taught first; details and exceptions afterwards." To bother children with rules for the formation of the plural, and to require them to learn by heart lists of exceptions which they already know through colloquial usage, seems to me a perverse attempt to make difficult what is easy, and to disgust children with what is, when properly taught, a pleasing, stimulating, and even amusing, exercise. You are entitled to ask for the plural of child, or ox, etc., but not to ask for a *list* of irregular plurals. This last is rote-

memory work. Many examination papers are constructed on this false principle, not only in schools, but in universities, and on other subjects than grammar.

8. *Gender* is in English a very easy matter. It is, however, better to use, for a time, the terms *male*, *female*, and *neither*, and to employ the word *kind* instead of the Latin term gender. I think you may, without danger to the child's intellectual and moral progress, omit the feminine of "Landgrave" and certain other words of this class.

9. The knowledge up to this time acquired by the pupil—and I use the word *acquired* advisedly, for it has not been put into him, but brought out of himself by himself, with your guidance and co-operation—having been thoroughly revised, the pupil is now in a position to name the class of each of the words in four or five lines of the reading-lesson of the day. Occasionally he should transfer these to the slate in columns. From day to day also he is adding to his stock of prepositions and conjunctions as he meets with them, and these he inserts in his note-book. He may now learn the distinction between proper and common nouns, but further distinctions should be scrupulously avoided. The salient and prominent are to take precedence of the rare and exceptional. Note that we are daily *turning to use* what has been acquired; and in order to maintain an intelligent connection with past teaching, and consequently the organic character of our teaching, we must be constantly going back, by the

help of the blackboard, to past introductory lessons, and thereby **testing intelligence.**

A short daily lesson during one **school term ought to bring a class composed of pupils in their** twelfth year as far as I have yet got. A fair familiarity with the parts of speech, the numbers and genders, **will now have** been obtained, and we then enter upon the **second** stage of grammar-teaching, which involves us **in syntax; and syntax is** unintelligible save as analysis.

Second Stage.

1. **What has hitherto been learned has been** taught on the basis of the sentence in **which** alone the function and consequent classification of words **find their concrete basis.**

You now, with a view **to** syntax, bring **more conspicuously forward** the knowledge the **pupil already has** of subject and predicate, thus:

> The child sleeps,
> **The** child cries,
> **The** child dresses her doll,

and so on. Keep always in mind the rule of method that generals **are to be formed** out of known particulars.

The verbs **having been named, you now** call **for the** difference **between** *cries* and *dresses*, **and** bring into view **the** fact of *transitive verb* **and** the *noun* as an *object*. And why? Because the verb does not **express by itself a complete** sense.

2. For the next week or two (taking care meanwhile to observe the memory rule of method and *daily to revise briefly all the child as yet knows*), you do nothing but exercise your pupils in this distinction of *subject* with *intransitive* verb as the principal word in the predicate, and *transitive* verb as the principal word in the predicate but requiring an object. In the course of these exercises, the change of form which the verb in the present tense undergoes, when we substitute a plural subject for a singular one, is apparent. We dwell on this step that we may obey the rule of Exactness as necessary to a sure and solid foundation for further knowledge.

Observe that at this stage we still continue to give the *whole* subject and the *whole* predicate, but we have now begun to distinguish the subject-noun and the object-noun. The words in italics in what follows are the whole subject: "*That fierce nation, the Goths, emerging with daring plans from the northern regions of Europe, armed with sword and spear,* advanced slowly but steadily southward."

Subject-noun and object-noun are the terms to be used instead of nominative and objective case.

I need not further illustrate this stage to those who have studied the analysis of sentences.

3. The pupil next "turns to use" all that he had been taught (thus revising and repeating); for he now parses sentences from his daily reading-lesson — that is to say, he names first the whole subject of a sentence and the whole predicate; he

then selects the predicative **verb**, and next the leading subject-noun, and the object-noun in relation to the verb when it is transitive. He then names each part of speech successively, points out the nouns which the adjectives qualify, also their number, gender, and so on. *The second term of the school year is now at an end.*

Third Stage.

1. You next direct the **pupil's** attention to the fact that the words called *prepositions*, which he has been gradually collecting in his note-book, do not make a complete sense any more than transitive verbs do, without an object; and you exercise him in this with the help of the blackboard, and embrace this piece of syntax in your parsing lessons henceforth.

2. When you enter on *tense*, you follow the rule that in teaching vernacular grammar you are raising vague and implicit knowledge to clear and explicit knowledge, by beginning thus: "When you leave school you say, 'I go home;' but you left school yesterday also, and would you say, 'I go home yesterday'? To-morrow also you will leave school, and you say, 'I shall go home to-morrow.'" They know the tenses *implicitly* already, and you are now simply raising the vagueness of the implicit to the clearness of the explicit; the word *time* being always used instead of the word *tense*. Every fresh step is to be written on the board, and in some cases, as in that of time, illustrated to the eye.

But only present, past, and future should at this stage be taught. All this will carry you well into the third school term; for an endless variety of simple exercises are needed at this stage, and you cannot go fast. (Step by step: little by little: be exact: repeat.) Moreover, remember that you are parsing daily as far as the pupil can parse, and so applying all the knowledge as yet acquired.

3. Observe now that the pupil has been gradually, as the result of his own observation, acquiring a few general rules of Syntax, viz.: "A verb agrees with its subject-noun;" "A transitive verb and a preposition require an object-noun." These, after they have been inscribed on the blackboard, should be written out by him in his note-book.

4. You now decline the pronouns, introducing them in connection with the verbs and not by themselves: thus, *you* say, "*I* learn my lesson," but if you are speaking *to* another you say—what? "*You* learn your lesson." [Here explain about "thou" as the true-singular.] If speaking of another you say, "He or she learns his or her lesson."

In this way you pick out the personal pronouns and write them out fully declined on the board, and get the pupils to copy them down in their note-books with a view to a home lesson.

5. The pupil is then led to extend his knowledge of time or tense and then moods, you using such words as telling-mood, commanding-mood, "may"-mood. You work out the verb in all its tenses and moods on the

blackboard in the same way, *i.e.* by drawing them out of the children, and getting them, after a few slate exercises, to write them out in tabular form in their note-books.

A thorough knowledge of the above course gives a child as extended and definite a knowledge of the foundations of grammar as any boy or girl need have. Revise and re-revise, and apply the knowledge in every possible way; always forcing your way through words to realities; *e.g.* gender is *kind*, singular is *single*, verb is *word*, tense is *time*. Use these words indifferently, or repeat them; *e.g.* "What time or tense is it?"

You will have observed that I have assumed that you teach orally by the aid of the blackboard and the ordinary lesson-book only, the child making notes in his book, and, in point of fact, constructing a Grammar for himself. But you yourself should be guided by some little text-book: this for the sake of the exercises, and as a relief to your own mind and memory.

The pupil has now reached his thirteenth year (twelve complete), and may have some cheap text-book put into his hands. I speak of the mass of children. He will now, at the beginning of his second year, very quickly run over the text-book with you; revising all he has acquired in one term: but the chief *addition* to his knowledge in doing so will be in the relative pronouns. There is really little or nothing more to do except to confirm what has been already acquired by means of a daily brief exercise. The pupil will now begin a foreign language with confidence, while daily parsing his English and extending his knowledge of analysis, step by step and slowly.

But let me beseech you not to go beyond what is called general analysis. Analysis of sentences is unquestionably overdone. The value of it will be found to consist in the correct application of a little *thoroughly known*. For example, if a boy, even at fourteen, can readily distinguish the enlargement of the subject, the extension of the predicate, the principal and subordinative clauses, the noun clause, the adnoun clause, and the adverb clause, he knows the logical organisation of a complex sentence, and this is enough.[1] Avoid minute distinctions which confuse, and by confusing the mind subvert discipline and draw attention away from the broader and more uniform relations of clauses; but take care that the boy is thoroughly familiar with the broader relations, and ready in discriminating them. I need scarcely say that analysis, like ordinary grammar, should be extracted from sentences by the pupil with your help, not learned from a book. I am disposed to think that the tabulating or pigeon-holing of the different clauses, and the use of symbols, should not be encouraged. The function of every clause in a complex sentence should be worked out in its relation to the meaning of the sentence as a whole and as a reality. In the writing out of tables there is too much of formulation, and the pupil becomes the slave of formulæ to such an extent that he parts company

[1] The clauses should always be named in these *grammatical* terms as far as possible. It is grammar, not logic, that we are teaching.

with the real, and, strange to say, may turn out a very good tabulated exercise, and yet have no conception of the *real* relations of the parts of the sentence.

The purpose you have in view must never be lost sight of. It is a disciplinary purpose; but besides this, and chiefly, you wish to increase the boy's power of seeing through the meaning of long and complex sentences, especially in poetry, and so extending his grasp and comprehension of literary language. You have the further practical purpose of giving him a more exact grasp of the language he himself daily uses, with the view to his employing it in his set compositions.

As a help it might be well to draw up a wall-sheet of the chief points in grammar and analysis to be constantly referred to. Do not buy somebody else's wall-sheet. I do not know what may be best in training mechanical engineers, but, in general education, the master and his boys should not only make the machine, but also their own tools as they need them.

Historical grammar may occasionally be referred to by yourself to illustrate peculiarities, such as ox*en*, kine, etc.; but no historical grammar should be formally taught before the age of fifteen, and even then very sparingly. If you attempt it in the early stages of study, you will hopelessly confuse the child's mind. His business is to learn what *is*, and not either what was, or may be, or will be.

I have not spoken of the whole of grammar. It

would be an insult to the intellect of teachers were I to enter into details of method over the whole field.

The importance of method, moreover, in abstract subjects lies in the initiation into the subject, the laying of the foundations of the new knowledge in its organic relations to what is already known—already in the mind of the pupil.

The principal defects found in the teaching of grammar in schools is, *first*, the piecemeal character of the teaching. The teacher forgets that every sentence is an organism to be taken to pieces and built up again as a living logical statement. *Secondly*, want of accuracy and precision, which prevails to a scandalous extent. This defect manifestly vitiates the whole teaching, and makes it worse than useless. The importance of grammar, remember, for boys and girls lies in this, that it is a valuable exercise of mind in analysis and in the discrimination of verbal distinctions and relations. It thus cultivates the power of distinguishing in general; and, above all, of distinguishing between things which are objects of reflection (notional), and not merely the more easily distinguished things of external observation. Now, if the distinctions made cross each other, or are vague and indefinite, parsing and analysis of sentences are illusory as a discipline. And, again, however accurate the distinctions may be, if they are too numerous, they defeat their own end by confusing the pupil.

Grammatical teaching, I have said, can have only three possible objects in a school—the formal discipline of mind, the more thorough understanding of reading-lessons, and the art of composition. The first is not only not promoted, it is unquestionably retarded, by vagueness of definition or the slurring over of difficulties; the second and third are not to be attained by mere parsing, unless it take the form of analysis, and be supported by actual practice in the construction of sentences and paragraphs.

Merely "fair" results in a subject of a formal kind, be it grammar or logic or mathematics, are of little practical value, disciplinary or other.

In conclusion, let the teacher, or the man of science who does not always fully appreciate grammar, consider for a moment the mental processes a boy is putting himself through when he parses a sentence, and he will see that there is in intelligent and accurate parsing a true discipline of the understanding. Take one of the simplest exercises—the parsing of "shall have seen." The boy first selects the word to which the others are auxiliary, referring it to a class in respect of the function it discharges in the sentence—a process first of analysis and then of deductive reasoning; he refers the auxiliary portions to their proper "time," —an act of discrimination among possible times or tenses; he relates the whole to its antecedent subject and its sequent object, which involves a perception of relations among separate thoughts and symbols of thoughts. Each successive word attacked is, in truth, a separate problem; and it is this characteristic which gives a subject of school instruction disciplinary value.

Realise this, and you cannot fail to realise at the same time the importance of the exercise and the necessity for exactness. Analysis of sentences is a repetition of the same kind of intellectual process in relation to the clauses of a complex sentence as that which we apply to words alone in ordinary parsing.

On this special branch of grammatical teaching known as analysis of sentences, I have not time here to do more than repeat what I have already said: It should be restricted within narrow limits; and, secondly, the terms applied to words should also be applied to clauses, viz. noun, adnoun or adjective, adverb, etc.

In dealing with grammatical teaching, I have been restricting myself to the upper-primary school, which begins at the age of eleven.

If pupils continue at school during the strictly secondary period of instruction, fourteen to seventeen or eighteen, the formal grammatical studies find their completion in historical grammar and the elements of comparative philology; but the *elements* only. By this time both boys and girls have some knowledge of two or three languages, and whether it be Romance or Teutonic or Classical philology which we teach, we are exercising the young scholar in scientific work—work as scientific in all its aspects as physics—more scientific in the large sense than chemistry or zoology. No man is a competent linguistic teacher in a secondary school who has not made a study of the comparative science of language. But bear in mind that the teaching of comparative philology and the genesis of English is not instruction in the English language, but a teaching of the science of language as illustrated by the particular case of English—a most interesting study, but a science like any other science, and to be taught only when it ought to be taught.

About the age of sixteen, boys and girls who have had a good foundation laid, begin to reason actively, and are not only fit for inductive and deductive scientific studies, but, if *these are kept within due limits*, they are attracted by them. Here, as everywhere else, all depends on the teacher, on his fulness of knowledge and on his method. Anglo-Saxon, etc., belong to the university stage of instruction. In the school they are out of place. Text-books of comparative grammar and rules, got up and applied *deductively*, reduce the elements of even this subject, naturally so fresh and stimulating, to the dreariness and aridity which characterised all teaching in the past, and afflict very much of it now.

In grammar, as in everything else, let us remember that the desire to attain to a measurable result in acquisition is ruinous. What we should aim at is a natural and pleasing activity of intelligence in the direction and on the lines of the various subjects we teach. Let us have quality, and quantity will take care of itself. This, I think, is certain, that if we fail to arouse intellectual interest and a voluntary and happy mental activity in connection with the subjects we teach, either we are, as educators, entirely on the wrong track, or our pupils are hopelessly stupid.

It is true that there are some things boys must learn, whether they can be led to take a living interest in them or not. Out of this compulsory learning arises a certain discipline and training of the commonplace boy in submission to conventionality and external rule, which lead to the formation of a safe habit of mind, and help to make him a respectable law-abiding citizen when he grows up—a result not to be despised. I fully recognise this; but my business in these lectures is to speak of education in its true living sense, as an inner movement of mind from ignorance to knowledge; and, were I dealing with moral education, I would add, from anarchy of feeling to ordered character.

LECTURE VIII.

LANGUAGE AS LITERATURE.

The third claim which language makes as a subject of instruction in the school is, that as literature it gives æsthetic culture. Here, as in preceding lectures, we speak of our native tongue alone.

As *substance* of thought, language instructs and fills the mind of youth with the words of wisdom, with the material of knowledge, and guides it to the meaning and motives of a rational existence, and while doing all this, it at the same time trains the intelligence: as a *formal* study, it further disciplines the intelligence, and gives vigour and discriminative force to intellectual operations in all the relations of the human mind to things, and therefore to the conduct of life: as *literature*, in which aspect we would now regard it, language cultivates, by opening the mind to a perception of the beautiful in form and the ideal in thought and action. It does this by bringing the prosaic truths of goodness and duty into the sphere of the idea, and so evoking and directing those aspirations, inherent in reason, which find their highest expression in spiritual realities.

In an excellent paper by Mr. Courthope-Bowen I find the following remark: "If we were to inquire in any hundred English schools, taken at random, whether literature formed a part of the regular school course, I think we should get positive, very positive, answers in the affirmative from at least ninety-nine. And yet I am prepared to maintain that at least ninety-eight of the ninety-nine answers would be wrong." I believe Mr. Courthope-Bowen to be right, and I say the same of Scottish schools. Chaucer's "Prologue" torn to bits, or a drama overlaid with Clarendon Press notes,—this is what schoolmasters too often call literature.

The question, What is literature as distinguished from the straightforward, logical, and lucid expression of thought? is, like the question, "What is poetry?" one excessively difficult to answer. One thing is certain—that literary expression is not merely grammatical and logical and fit expression, but "beautiful" expression. We are here in the domain of Rhetoric. Thus far all may agree, and we may amble out of the difficulty on that skittish and bright-winged Pegasus, "the Beautiful," leaving each man to attach to the word his own more or less vague conceptions, but always more or less definite *feelings*. The Renaissance, as we know, restored to men the perception and enjoyment of the beautiful in language; and we do not misjudge the apostles of the Revival if we say that in their conviction the most beautiful language always embodied the highest thoughts and the deepest realities of life.

Barbarisms in Latin or Greek meant barbarisms and crudities in thought. The inevitable result of this view was that men strove after eloquence and elegance of expression, and, ere long, style governed all. Now, to cultivate style for style's sake is the pharisaism of the intellect. The great masters of style, Sophocles, Euripides, Dante, Shakespeare, Milton, did not do this. With them, as with all writers who live in the esteem of generations, thought comes first, and style is nothing more than the apt and felicitous expression of prior thought. Style is not to be compared to the vesture which covers a man's body, but rather to the native and natural covering of the beasts of the field. The play and elasticity of the close-fitting lion's hide is very different from any vestment with which the fashionable tailor covers the lion's master. In fact, a beautiful thought and a beautiful expression either occur as *one* in a man's mind, or the thought remains as a vague possibility or anticipation only (on the plane of mere feeling), until it finds fitting words. At this point a man, to use the words of Montaigne, is only "licking the formless embryo of thought." When the thought is born, it is born with its natural vestment. It is that natural vestment which, looked at apart from the thought, we call style.

My business here and now, however, is not with the principles of literary æsthetics, but only with so much of the literary, in contradistinction to the merely grammatical, as concerns the education of boys and girls. And I have said enough in my first lecture to show that you cannot bring a pupil to the perception and appreciation of a beautiful and felicitous phrase without admitting him thereby to the comprehension of the beautiful and felicitous thought. I have endeavoured in past pages to show that it is through words that we educate to things, for words are the records of the past conquests of humanity over things: they have been called "the fortresses of thought;" and but for them, each generation would have to begin all over again, and barbarism would be permanent. Words are the title-deeds of the inheritance of each child of man. So also in the æsthetic sphere, it is by dwelling on beautiful language, and learning to appreciate it, that we reach the beauty of the reality —the thought.

Whatever may be the definition of literature, it is incumbent on us to find out, if we can, its relation to the ethical aim of education. I am disposed to put it thus:—

The true man of genius, as opposed to the *littérateur*, who lives by simply borrowing the clothes of the great, and wearing them in a flaunting free and easy way as if they had been made for him, is always in search of the "idea." Do not conclude, however, that all who are in search of the idea are men of genius. The idea simply means the perfected truth of things, and of each thing—be it the law of the stars, the law of the animal organism, or the "truest truth" of the encounter of man's mind with nature and human life. This truth, put in a concrete form, is the ideal within its own sphere. Hence the paradox, the ideal is the real; for the idea is the ultimate truth, and the ultimate truth is the sole reality. What Lord Bacon, in a well-known passage, says of the highest form of literature is true, in due degree, of all literature. "Poetry," he says, "doth raise and erect the mind by submitting the shows of things to the desires of the mind, whereas reason doth buckle and bow the mind unto the nature of things." This aim of poetry does not weaken the mind, as Plato would seem to say, but admits us to the truth and reality of things by admitting us to their idea, to which Plato would force an entrance by means of philosophy. Doubtless there are some nations whose youth would be best trained by the prosaic teachings of hard fact and the severe discipline of science; but the British nation is certainly not one of these. By converse with literature in its purest forms we elevate the character without weakening it. Nay, elevation is itself strength.

Without dwelling longer on this question than is necessary for my purpose, let me now assume that literature—the beautiful in expression—is the ideal. It is the striving after the highest and truest truth of things finding at last fit utterance. As in the pursuit of the idea, so in the contemplation of it, there is a large element of emotion. There is an excitement of feeling which intellect by itself could not give.

Pass now, then, to the minds of boys and girls when,

after they have reached the age of puberty, there begins to be felt the underground swell of ethical emotion, and, along with this, the intellectual tendency to idea and ideals. We as educators have to meet, to satisfy, to direct this into proper channels. Several agencies suggest themselves, but I here speak only of language. It is at this point in the growth of a mind that language as literature exhibits its supreme power as an instrument in the hands of a sensible teacher.

Grant this; yet the result of all converse with literature, it may be said, is, after all, only an æsthetic result. It adds to the happiness of life, and increases the pleasures of the imagination. This is a desirable thing, as all legitimate pleasure is, but it is not essential to a good life, nor even to a noble and heroic life. True so far: art is not ethics; but it is precisely because it contributes so powerfully to ethical culture, that I beg the teacher to take possession of art in literary form as the most potent of all subsidiary agencies at every stage of school life, and especially in the critical years of adolescence: nothing is so formative.

The state of the spiritual, as opposed to the merely moral, man is, I suppose, that the former lives in ideas and the ideal as the true and ultimate expression of the reason of man—as the God-given reality of his nature. Ideas may be said to be the thought of God in man,—the "words that proceed out of the mouth of God;"—and by living in ideas we truly live in Him and with Him. So seductive, indeed, is the spiritual life—the life in ideas, so much does it transcend the merely moral and juridical relations of the hearth and the market-place, that men of strong spiritual tendencies have been, as history abundantly shows, frequently led to regard the ordinary duties of the family and the State as superseded by spiritual emotions and ideal aspirations. There are probably very few strongly spiritual natures which, owing to this tendency, have not had at some period of their lives a serious fall. They have forgotten that man's feet are on earth, and that the true ideal is the ideal of the ordinary and the commonplace, and, as such, the true real. "In this poor hampered Actual, here or nowhere is this ideal," says Carlyle. Certain natures are apt to forget that all idealism of emotion, all religious aspiration, is spurious except in so far as it grows out of the soil of the domestic and civic virtues, and is dominated by law. It is a spurious ideal which transcends duty: the true ideal is always the recognition of law — the true and ultimate law of our nature. As a matter of metaphysical fact, the spiritual life, the life in ideas, the life in God, bears the same relation to the *real* of common duty as the abstract in the sphere of the purely intellectual bears to the real and concrete of things. Except in so far as the general and abstract is seen in particular things, except in so far as things are seen in the general and abstract, both are, in their isolation, unmeaning and unfruitful: and what is true in the sphere of knowledge is equally true in the sphere of life and conduct.

It is only after he has reached the age of puberty that a youth begins to be alive to ideas, and it is generally at the end of the secondary period of instruction—about the age of eighteen—that they begin to take possession of him as potent factors in his life. It would almost seem as if many boys and girls, and men and women, are constitutionally unfitted for ideal conceptions, and consequently for the ideal in living. But this is a wrong way of looking at the actual facts. The finer organisations, by their innate force, pass from the preceptive morality of the boy-life into the ideal life of adolescence without effort and without teaching. The mass have the capacity but not the inner impulse. They have to be educated into it. The passage from the one mental condition into the other is what old theological writers described as conviction and conversion and regeneration. This it is to be born again. This is, fundamentally, Christianity. This is to escape from the schoolmaster, the law, into the freedom of the spirit, from morality into spirituality. It is the perception of the intrinsic worth and beauty of the ethical as itself in itself aim and end of life. Are parents and teachers to let this transformation come or not *as it pleases?* If so, then I ask what I have asked before, What do they mean by education, and why do they educate at all?

If you think that physical science will work this regenerative change, you are mistaken. How to promote it is a difficult and delicate question.

But however difficult and delicate it may be, it

is our duty to try to solve it, and to look about among the materials of school education and see if we can find an instrument suited to our purpose. Direct instruction in the dogmas of religion and in spiritual truths does not seem often to succeed. Now, in language as literature, we shall find the instrument we want; for literature is the æsthetic expression of ideas, and by habituating the mind to live in this ideal atmosphere we predispose it to all things spiritual. We do not call forth the antagonism of the young mind by dogmatically repressing its growing self-assertiveness, and trying to overawe it. We would rather counterbalance it by giving it an objective and universal outlook. We turn the eye of the mind to contemplate what is beautiful, and to enjoy it; and Plato truly tells us that with the eye the whole mind turns, and not merely a part of it. We thus insensibly lead the human spirit by green pastures into the life in ideas; and we believe that that life will then move forward by its own innate force of aspiration, its own inherent vitality, until it has become the conscious life in God—the religious life.

The criticism of language as literature belongs chiefly to the latter half of the secondary period; and it is not till a boy is sixteen at least that I should endeavour, *of set purpose*, to interest him in the self-conscious literature for its own sake as an ideal expression of human life.

But it does not follow from this that we are not to bring the young mind face to face with literature before the secondary school stage. Even in the infant school we begin our work. In this, as in everything else in education, we begin at the beginning. The simple verses which give fit and sweet expression to simple childlike thoughts, are to be read and learned by heart. What is not literature, in the best sense, to us, is literature to a child. Every stage of mental life has its literature; and at each stage, as one succeeds another, we take care that the prose and poetry set before the child are, though simple, good of their kind. We take care, further, that he understands; and by our own good reading of the pieces, and by requiring them to be learned by heart, we gradually make our pupils *feel* the good in literary expression. We seek, in fact, for many years simply to make *impressions* of the right kind, deferring criticism, that is to say, the conscious discrimination of the apt and beautiful, until a later period. In religious education all surely feel how important it is that gooood hymns be learned and sung by children. Hymns, aided by the simple story of the life of Christ, will together accomplish more for the religious education of the young than all the catechisms and church-going in the world. I might illustrate this; but I am dealing with literature as part of secular instruction only, if indeed there be such a thing as secular instruction. Let me give one or two pieces which belong to the child stage :—

Take Hood's "Past and Present"—

> "I remember, I remember,
> The house where I was born,"

the last stanza of which runs thus:—

> "I remember, I remember,
> The fir-trees dark and high;
> I used to think their slender tops
> Were close against the sky;
> It was a childish ignorance,
> But now 'tis little joy
> To know I'm further off from heaven
> Than when I was a boy."

This now is retrospective, and therefore may be said to anticipate the experience of a child; but I am far from thinking this an objection in a piece so easily understood as regards language. It is sufficiently understood at the time of learning, and it comes back after many days. Pieces which have a certain lilt and alliteration about them are well suited to children. For example:—

> "The cock is crowing,
> The stream is flowing,
> The small birds twitter,
> The lake doth glitter,
> The green field sleeps in the sun;
> The oldest and youngest
> Are at work with the strongest;
> The cattle are grazing,
> Their heads never raising;
> There are forty feeding like one.
> Like an army defeated,
> The snow hath retreated."
> Etc. etc. (WORDSWORTH.)

Take again Mrs. Hemans' "Child's First Grief," which I need not quote. Then Wordsworth's "Robin:"—

> "Art thou the bird whom man loves best,
> The sweet bird with the scarlet breast,
>   Our little English Robin—
> The bird that comes about our doors
> When autumn winds are sobbing?
>
> . . . . . .
>
> The bird that by some name or other
> All men who know thee call thee brother?"

Keble's "Book of Nature," Logan's "Cuckoo," Wordsworth's "Lucy Gray," "Alice Fell," and "Pet Lamb," and Tennyson's "May Queen," and many others of this class, at once suggest themselves. All these, with the best of Longfellow's poems, not to speak of the riches of ballad literature, national songs (see also "The Children's Garland," by Palgrave), the natural and breezy poetry of Scott, and good prose pieces, will fill the waking mental life of a boy up to the age of fifteen, till he, "by ever dwelling on great thoughts, becomes like greatest men." The "Iliad" and "Odyssey" in English might be read, and the Arthurian cycle now or a little later.

Up to this point—the age of fifteen or so—we have been daily guiding the pupil in making acquaintance with words, that through them he may know *things*—the things of thought, the things that determine conduct. Mind and language have been growing together. Our main object has been the nutrition and training of mind through language as a Real. Formal discipline of intelligence through grammar (in the large sense in which we have used that term) we have not neglected, but we have always subordinated it to the claims of the Real. The pupil now not only comprehends language in a wide and various range, but he can use it for the expression, if not always of his own thoughts, yet for the reproduction with grammatical correctness of the thoughts of others. But in addition to all this, he has, if wisely educated, received in abundance, literary *impressions* from simple and good poetry, and these have been gradually moulding his life.

Mr. R. L. Nettleship, in expounding Plato, speaks of the influence of plastic art on the young—the productions of those men who "have the genius to track out the nature of what is fair and shapely," and to embody it in their works. Young citizens, he says, "should be like men living in a beautiful and healthy place; from everything that they see and hear, loveliness, like a breeze, should pass into their souls and teach them, without their knowing it, the truth of which it is a manifestation." What is true of the plastic arts is still more true of literature.

But now we may venture a step further, and go beyond mere impressions. We have reached the epic stage, for we are dealing with the period during which action and heroism best meet the wants of the boy of wholesome nature. Readings of this kind in prose and poetry must mainly be relied on if we are to educate; Shakespeare and such pieces as those contained in "Lyra Heroica,"[1] also Plutarch's "Lives," and well-selected historical readings. But we may go further than mere reading, especially in prose and poetry of the concise and abstract character. We may attend, not merely to the analysis of the thought, but to the beauty of expression, and its felicity in conveying the complex emotions of human experience, or, it may be, its failure to do so. We do not at this stage part with our past training and discipline: we carry it with us into the higher literary exercise. It all helps us to see that aptness of phrase, balance of rhythm, grace of structure, are not by themselves good literature; that, on the contrary, the inner truth of the thing before us, and its logical coherence, are the necessary foundations of the best literary art.

It will be said, by a few, that this is to turn the young mind into the field of literary criticism—a premature occupation. It certainly is literary criticism of a sort, because it is an attempt to see in what respects the piece of prose or poetry before us is good or bad, or middling. But why should a growing mind be asked to accept phrases for realities, a jingle of words for truth, a sensuous blotch for nature, and be arbitrarily arrested in its natural desire to discriminate between the good and bad, and so gradually to form its own standard of the fit and true? Is not the very object of education to guide

[1] By W. E. Henley.

and help the action of mind in its successive stages of comprehension of all that the various world presents to its experience, either directly or through the interpretation furnished by other and greater minds? This is the "criticism of life."

Doubtless such literary exercises may be overdone, or misdirected. Everything depends on the teacher. In the hands of a pedant they will become pedantic; in the hands of a fool they will be foolish; in the hands of a fanatic who can appreciate only one form of art—to whom Keats is perfection, and Wordsworth prosy and nothing more—they will be one-sided and misleading. But not so much harm will be done, even in these circumstances, as the good that will result from rousing the interest, and stimulating the activity, of mind, to the apprehension of ideal forms.

Perhaps I may illustrate from a personal experience, not three weeks old, what I mean by an elementary literary exercise. I was in a remote country school frequented by boys and girls, the children of ploughmen and crofters. The highest class, composed of five boys and four girls, of the average age of thirteen, had read to me a piece selected from their class-book by myself, but already partially known to them—Longfellow's "Building of the Ship." When they had finished, it occurred to me to say, "Now, instead of troubling ourselves about the subject and predicate and extension and all the rest of it, go to your seats, sit apart from each other, read the poem carefully to yourselves, compare one part with another, and mark the lines you think the most beautiful." They did so, and it was to me, as an educationalist, a pleasant sight to see the intentness of countenance with which these rough and awkward country lads and lasses applied themselves to this, their first lesson in literary criticism. After about ten minutes had elapsed, I called for their opinions. One boy and one girl had selected lines which suggested sadness; the remaining three girls had selected those which had reference to marriage—the bride and bridegroom; a second boy selected the most striking image, while the remaining three had selected the lines which had to do with intense action. Each read aloud the part which he had selected; when this was over, I made a few conversational remarks on one or two points in the poem suggested by their own selections. These they listened to with avidity, because they were now *prepared* to listen. This is what I call a *literary* lesson; and I shall be much surprised to learn that any teacher does not see how much more educative and fruitful this simple and natural and conversational treatment of a piece of good prose or poetry must be, than any amount of sentence-analysis; or even (shall we say?) of Latin grammar.

I know that some will say, " Do not be in a hurry; all the needed appreciation of literature, and the culture and the ideas its brings with it, will come in time." My conviction is that they will *not* come, any more than religion comes of itself, or a scientific habit of mind comes of itself. Is it not notorious that, as a matter of fact, they do not come? In language as literature we have to begin, as in all other subjects, low down. We have to lay the foundations early, and let them settle, if we are to build on them to any good purpose. In everything Plato's remark is true, that man, of all animals, stands most in need of education, and is the most capable of being educated. Setting aside the exceptional boy, it is certain that if I suddenly introduce a boy of sixteen or seventeen, who has had no previous education in the language of literature and no training in feeling its beauties, to Wordsworth or Milton, I shall fail to interest him. So is it in other studies: I should fail to interest the same boy in a truly *scientific* book on Physics, or Geology, if I had not planted and daily nurtured in him a habit of interest in nature, directing his attention to its more ordinary and superficial phenomena, and to the explanation of these. I speak, of course, of the ordinary boy, which means ninety-five per cent. of boys. With boys of genius the educator has little to do, save to guide and control. It is notorious that the mass of boys said to be educated take no interest in nature; and if we add to this that they take no interest in pure literature,—that is to say, in the best thoughts of the best of their own race expressed in fitting form,—what is the use of all our educational machinery? Surely there is a blunder somewhere. I am not such a cynic as to believe that the human animal is so constructed by his Maker, as to have a natural aversion to the contemplation of the beautiful and various world in its causes and harmonies, and to the perusal of the greatest thoughts on things and men as these are finely expressed by the prophets and seers of his race.

It follows from what has been said that at all stages of language-teaching we should read largely. At the stage of which we are now speaking, our reading must be varied and liberal, with a view to fill a boy's mind with masterpieces. This is what the teaching of English literature in the school ought to be. And by such teaching the boy may, perchance, be gradually led, as Plato thought, to recognise the forms of goodness through what is presented to sense and imagination.

As regards Method, we have done little as yet but apply the great rule that a subject should be begun from the beginning, and, as we proceed, be brought into fit relation with the stage of mental progress the pupil has reached. Step *by* step, step *after* step. In truth, however, there is scarcely a rule of method which is not as applicable to the teaching of literature as to the teaching of any other subject. Only one is a little averse to be guilty of the pedantry of applying them in detail. For in the domain of literature, as in that of religion, it may be said that rules of procedure, which may be of great use to a teacher in matters of the pure intellect, are of little value unless he is himself inspired. The genuine love of literature, the sympathetic living with the growing minds of the young, and the impulse to give to others that which enriches your own **life and which** you further enrich yourself by giving, supersede **all rules of method.** Still, a word or two may be **profitably said in correction** of obvious faults, although the result **be merely** negative.

Here let me quote again from Mr. Courthope-Bowen: "**By** the study **of** literature as *literature*, I mean the study of a poem or prose-work for the sake of its substance, its form, and its style; for the sake of the thought and imagination **it** contains, and the methods used to express these; **for the** sake of **its** lofty, large, or acute perception of things; its power of exposition; the beauty, force, and meaning of its **metaphors, its similes, its epithets; the** strength **and music of** its language." I quote this because I think **it well** said, and also because it describes the working of the second governing rule of all method, "**Let your** process be analytico-synthetic." **To work this out in** detail is not my intention, but **you** will find most of the suggestions for teaching a piece of prose **as substance** of thought, applicable also in the sphere of pure literature.

As a matter of fact, it is notorious that many schoolmasters cannot shake off their hardness, their formalism, their **pedantry, in** this field of instruction any more than in that of religion; and the result is that literature in the school resolves itself into a list of **literary** names and **dates,** and **sinks into the** examination of words, and **of** grammatical and historical forms and facts. A play of Shakespeare or Milton's "Lycidas" is read with a view to its anatomy, not to what the poems convey to the intellect and emotions — the satisfaction of the ideal in man. In the editions used the product of the artist is lost in a monstrous superfetation of notes. Why do so many teachers make *lessons* of everything?

Thus it is that the majority of boys at this secondary school stage care nothing for books, except books of impossible adventure or comic presentations of serious things. In these they find relief from the dissection of a great writer, whether the writer be English or Latin or Greek. And they are justified in the course they take. How can we expect any one to enjoy "Lycidas," or Portia's speech, or Hamlet's soliloquy, or Tintern Abbey, or the Ode to Duty, if they read ten lines a day, have to learn by heart a lot of notes (philological or antiquarian), and then begin to mangle the passages by constructing parsing and analysis tables — finally, perhaps, resorting to the degrading process of paraphrasing? This would be to expect an impossibility. You, the teacher, are ostensibly giving him literature, whereas truly you are cheating him and giving him grammar—words, words, words. You are ostensibly giving him the real of literature; you are truly palming off upon him the formal and abstract. I would rather have the exclusive Latin training back again in all its aridity. There are plenty of *corpora vilia* in the English tongue on which the dreary experiments of grammar and analysis may be made. But be honest here, and if you affect to give him literature, give him literature. For one boy who enters with spirit into the formal, there are ten who appreciate the real, and five who appreciate the beautiful. And is it not evident that, if out of a class of forty boys we can send out even thirty inspired by the great writings of great men, we have educationally accomplished far more for them than by sending them out with the most exact notions of grammar and analysis, while dead to literature? If we have ever realised to ourselves that the final aim of all education, both of the school and the world, is an ethical aim, we cannot doubt this for a moment.

Select then the books which are within the comprehension of your class, and read them liberally, generously. There is a superabundance of English literature of this class, not to speak of good translations from other languages. Then, read the books *with* the pupils. Let *them* read, and do you also take your turn of reading. Enjoy the book together —not as a lesson, but as a pleasant symposium. This is the sum and substance of the method. When you come to a particularly fine passage, direct attention to it, ask them to point out its artistic beauties, and then read it to them a second time as it ought to be read. That is to say, if you *can* read: it is not so easy to read well.

I do not mean to say that in such literary school-banquets you are to eschew all questionings. If a difficult phrase or allusion occur, ask in a friendly and conversational way what the precise force of it is: above all, let it be understood that *you are there to be questioned.* If it be poetry you are reading, encourage the boys to learn beautiful passages by heart, but avoid *prescribing* them. This is no task-work in which you are engaged. Says Quintillian (i. 8), "Point out the beauty of the arrangement, the charms of the subject-matter, the appropriateness of the words to the characters represented, what is worthy of praise in the substance, what in the words used," and so forth. It is now, if ever, that you are *living* with your boys. Now truly mind meets mind. It is now, and through this literary sympathy, that you lay deep the foundations of your moral influence on the whole future lives of your pupils. It is now that you are truly developing the religious possibilities of the little men and women before you. This, and not the spelling out with tears and vexation a dozen lines of Virgil, is the "Humanities."

The "practical" teacher, and most of all, strange to say, the Latin and Greek expert, who, because he "trades in classic niceties" and imitates felicitously, thinks he makes good his exclusive claim to the name of "Humanist," will tell me, "Ah! this is theory; you don't know boys: why, even with the best teaching, one-half of them would find all this a bore." To which I can only reply that I think I do know boys, and that if one-half of them find such intercourse as this with their master a bore, it is due to previous neglect of the real of thought and art, or to you the master. Perhaps you put on your gown and college cap, and come down on them with a magisterial air, and with the aspect of omniscience. Even the luminous charm of Tennyson, or the deep calm communings of Wordsworth, cannot drive the superiority and the pedantry out of you. Who would accept "Il Penseroso" out of the mouth of the parish beadle? You come to your class-room to teach these poets, forsooth! to patronise them, and, through them, your boys. Now, it is clear that this kind of work is too fine, too delicate for you; the college cap is out of place; the work must be done in your shirt-sleeves, if it is to be done at all. The boys are to lead and you are to follow. Pray, how much more do you know than your boys in this field? It will be a stupid class that cannot puzzle you in the first five minutes by its questions. And you are no true educator if you do not rejoice to be puzzled by them.

A certain percentage of inferior organisms will doubtless be found in every class, and they will get no good; but how much larger is the percentage who resist and reject your formal and grammatical teaching? And yet you go on with it, and rightly so, in its proper place, which, however, is not here in the sacred literary hour. Such things belong to the outer porch; we are now within the Temple of the Muses.

The question was recently debated in connection with Oxford University: Can Literature be taught?

It seemed to me that, as was natural in the case of university dons, the question was mixed up with a quite different one : Can Literature be examined on ? "Chatter about Shelley and Harriet"—this was the description of the essays that would be sent up for degrees. There is much truth in the criticism which the bitter phrase would convey. Literature as literature can never be a good *examination* subject; and if it could, it ought not to be so degraded as to be taught with a view to an examination. But it certainly can be taught—taught in the Infant school, and in the High school, and in the University, and all through life. Nor should any curriculum for an Arts degree be held to be adequate which does not include attendance on a course of literary history and criticism, as is the case in the Scottish Universities. Its relative place among other subjects for a degree can easily be arranged.

The man who doubts whether literature can be taught, must have strange notions of the meaning of the word teaching. Is it not one of the pleasantest occupations in the world to read a good piece of prose or poetry with a young and ardent mind, and, by dwelling on its true meaning and its beauties, to introduce that mind to the humanities, and thereby raise higher the plane of his daily life—spiritualising him by humanising him ? Why, then, is it not done ? The answer perhaps is, because it is very difficult to do. The teacher who will do the work successfully must be himself a man of humane culture, and of sympathy with the nascent and adolescent life of mind. If some so endowed have, notwithstanding, failed, it is because the foundations in the minds of their pupils, as I have said, have never been laid: the way has not been prepared. As summer is waning and autumn approaches, you hurry on with a view to a harvest, not only in literature, but in all that pertains to the spiritual life. You forgot to break up the soil in early spring, and to sow the seed, and to harrow. The warm summer sun consequently played ineffectually on a hard surface, and if anything has been produced at all, as will certainly be the case where the native qualities of the soil are worth anything, it is weeds or wild oats.

If you think it necessary in the later years of the secondary school to give some instruction in the history of literature, you will give it in connection with the history of your country. You will give the minimum number of dates and the maximum of inner real connections. When this is done, the reading of a narrative of English literature will at least do no harm. But read an author before you read about him; "Matter before Form." It is the extended reading in history and native literature that strengthens the patriotic spirit, out of which the highest expression of the national mind in words and acts can alone come.

Again I say, is it not the fact that the general result of all our education is that boys and girls, youths and maidens, do not, as a rule, even after they have grown up, read anything except narratives of events, real or imaginary, which have a power of exciting the mind? They care also, perhaps, for accounts of proposals that affect their own immediate material wellbeing. As regards literature, they are barbarians. Listen to the drawing-room songs that are sung and applauded. Are our upper classes—the pure product of the great Public Schools—really above the level of the Music Saloon? No use complaining of this; so it will be to the end of time, as regards a section of every population. But if an enjoyment of literature and a genuine interest in the beauties of various nature be the marks of a cultivated mind, then the culture and civilisation of a nation may be fairly measured by the *proportion* of the population who love literature and who have an open mind for the Divine show of things, and for the moral meaning of the world. This—not Latin and Greek—is the Humanities; Latin and Greek are the Humanities only in so far as they are this, and no further. As educationalists, our duty is to increase the proportion of those so humanised in each successive generation; and this, because the ethical life of a people is largely determined by their interest in such things. And I venture to affirm that, in the sphere of religion and morality, nothing can so surely promote and sustain purity of feeling, reasonableness of opinion, and elevation of standard, as love of literature and a sympathy with nature.

The extent to which such great results are attainable in the school depends on the conception which the teacher forms of his spiritual function, and the methods by which he gives effect to his conception. Let it not be supposed that I advocate the undue fostering of the emotional and ideal in youth. I merely wish to satisfy and direct a need and a capacity which God has given. No man is more profoundly convinced than I am that the education of the human spirit is not completed when it is merely permeated by feeling and elevated by emotion. Reason, whose function it is to raise into the sphere of absoluteness and duty the ideal teachings of emotion, must be disciplined and strengthened. The heart has to be subdued by the intellect, life and its purposes have to be rationalised by each for himself, and the vagueness of sentiment has to become the certitude of the science of conduct. Law must regulate and govern emotion, but it is law within the sphere of emotion and does not supersede it.

I have now dealt, as briefly as I could, with language in the school in its concrete, its formal, and its literary aspects. It is the mother-tongue of which I have been speaking, and I hope I have made it clear that no subject, or combination of subjects, approaches the mother-tongue as an educational instrument. It is the centre round which the life of every earnest mind revolves: it is the soil in which alone it can truly live; and *therefore* it is and must be the centre round which all true education of the young mind must revolve, the soil into which every growing mind must strike its roots deep, if its growth is to be vigorous, native, national, and humane.

I will now speak of foreign tongues and the method of teaching them, taking Latin as type.

LECTURE IX.

FOREIGN LANGUAGES—LATIN AS TYPE.

Reasons for Teaching Latin.

I HAVE already shown you that the best culture which a man receives through language is to be obtained only through his mother-tongue. While he *seems* to be deriving culture from a foreign language, it is in fact chiefly from the comparisons, similarities, contrasts of the forms of thought and expression in that language with the forms already familiar to him, that he receives intellectual and moral benefit and a finer æsthetic perception. The foreign tongue, accordingly, will be of substantial advantage in his education, apart from its practical uses, only in so far as he, more or less consciously, transmutes its forms, its thought, its images, its delicacies, into the familiar vernacular which is, and must always be, the vesture and expression of his own inner life. Language, as I have frequently said, is a necessity for the growth of mind. Growth depends on finding fit utterance for those complex mental states which succeed each other in the history of the race and of the individual, and are ever deepening their significance and widening their range. If the form or mould into which each man's mental life runs, and by means of which he feels and thinks as a self-conscious being, be his own vernacular, then Latin, Greek, or French, or German, can never be a substitute for this, but only contribute to its richness, explicitness, fulness, and fitness.

Now, fortunately, it is impossible to learn any foreign tongue whatsoever without the constant discrimination of difference and recognition of likeness as between that tongue and the vernacular, thus forcing the latter into clearer consciousness, and making us critical of our own utterances. The result is that native words, phrases, syntactical forms, metaphorical expressions, are no longer known and used by the student in a merely rote or imitative way, but with due regard to their true significance as symbols. And although to be conscious of language is not to be conscious of the processes of thought as such, it is the next thing to it; and thus a great step is made towards a thinking life of intelligence, as opposed to the rote, imitative, and conventional life of mind. Consciousness becomes self-consciousness. In brief, it is just because the conscious exercise of thought on the necessary vehicle of thought is the nearest approach to the exercising of thought on thought itself, that it is so highly educative, both as a training and as a discipline.

I select Latin as type of foreign tongues for many

reasons unnecessary to detail here. Our first question when we admit a subject to the school curriculum must always be, "*Why* do we teach it?" "It is the province of a teacher," says Mr. Thring, "to know why he teaches as well as what he teaches and how to teach." A modest demand to make of the teacher surely: is it an impertinence to suggest that, while still young and not yet hardened in scholastic vices, he should be trained to know all this?

Reasons for Teaching Latin.

Other reasons than those which influenced the fourteenth, fifteenth, and sixteenth centuries must be sought for. And there must be valid reasons which have operated powerfully on the side of natural conservatism; for mere conservatism itself could scarcely have done all that some attribute to it. Other reasons, and, it seems to me, sufficient reasons, there are.

I am not going to discuss the question whether a foreign language should be approached from the imitative or grammatical side. I shall content myself with giving, dogmatically, my own conclusion, reached in the light of the objects we have in view in teaching a foreign tongue, as well as of some experience. That conclusion is, that teaching in every foreign tongue should embrace the *grammatical*, or formal, side, and rest on it as its only sure foundation; but matter must always precede form.

The question remains, *How* is the grammar of the foreign tongue to be taught? The general answer must be, Just as English grammar is taught. The method which I explained and illustrated in the teaching of English grammar can be applied by any one, without extraneous help, to Latin or French or German, if he will only think it out. There are certain differences, it is true, but these generally arise out of the *specific reasons* for teaching this or that foreign tongue. Accordingly, I ask you to go with me into the reasons for teaching Latin in these modern times, and I shall then illustrate the method. I would only further premise that, as we have to approach a foreign tongue in such a way as to insure a knowledge of its grammar, it is impossible to separate the real from the formal in our instruction. These advance *pari passu*.

We teach Latin—

(1.) Because as a formal and grammatical study it has peculiar advantages, and, more effectually than any other language (except Greek),[1] gives discipline to the intelligence, and the result of discipline, viz. intellectual power.

(2.) The study of Latin gives (to an Englishman at least), more than any other language can do, a training in words—the relative values and the functions of words, and, consequently, training in the thought-things which words denote. The shades of meaning in vocables are brought into high relief.

---

[1] For *boys*, Greek is inferior to Latin, in my opinion, especially for British boys.

(3.) The analysis and subsequent synthesis whereby we truly comprehend an English sentence, and which is a direct training of the processes of mind in knowing (in the scientific or any other field), are most effective as training when it is a foreign tongue that we are teaching; and, above all, when that foreign tongue is Latin. This because, in order to give the English translation, a pupil is forced, whether he will or not, deliberately and of set purpose to consider the mutual relations of the parts of a complex sentence; and, secondly, because of the exactness and precision with which these logical relations are brought into prominence in a highly synthetic language. In this relation, Latin is better than Greek, because there is less deviation in it from a normal type. There is breadth, strength, and simplicity about its grammar. Let me here quote from Marmontel's *Mémoires d'un père*, etc.:—

"The choice and use of words, in translating from one language to another, and even then some degree of elegance in the construction of sentences, began to interest me; and this work, which did not proceed without the analysis of ideas, fortified my memory. I perceived that it was the idea attached to the word which made it take root, and reflection soon made me feel that the study of the languages was also the study of the art of distinguishing shades of thought, of decomposing it, of forming its texture, and of catching with precision its spirit and its relations; and that along with words, an equal number of new ideas were introduced and developed in the heads of the young, and that in this way the early classes were a course in elementary philosophy, much more rich, more extended, and of greater real utility than we think, when we complain that in our colleges nothing is learned but Latin." [1]

---

[1] From Prof. Payne's translation of Compagné's *History of Pedagogy*.

(4.) The working out of a translation from a foreign tongue is, further, a training of the imagination, which has to bring itself into play in order to unite into a whole, in their true signification, the parts of a sentence. Latin in a special sense gives this training because of its remoteness. The imagination, moreover, is checked and kept within the wholesome bounds of truthfulness by comparing the result achieved with the original.

(5.) Latin is, to a very large extent (to the extent of two-thirds at least), our own tongue. In studying Latin, therefore, we are studying our own tongue in its sources, and getting all the discipline and nutrition of mind which flows from the study of the origin and *history* of words. Latin enables us to revivify our own tongue for ourselves. Nay, we are studying our own language in much of its syntactical mould also, as may be seen by reading our early prose writers, and even those of the eighteenth century.

(6.) It follows from the preceding reason, that, in studying Latin, we are brought face to face with modern conceptions as to moral duties, social relations, and legal obligations *in their origins*, and that we thus undergo a kind of unconscious philosophical training suited to the, as yet, immature mind, and moulding its conceptions from the foundation. Dr. W. T. Harris, Education Commissioner for the United States, says:—

"One may say that of a hundred boys, fifty of whom had studied Latin for a period of six months, while the other fifty had not studied Latin at all, the fifty with a smattering of Latin would possess some slight impulse towards analysing the legal and political view of human life, and surpass the other fifty in this direction. Placed on a distant frontier with the task of building a new civilisation, the fifty with the smattering of Latin would furnish law-makers and political rulers, legislators, and builders of the State."

This may be an exaggeration, but there is an element of truth in it. In any case, Latin is not a dead language. Its influence is still living in our own tongue, our thought, our feeling, our institutions, our law, our religion, our policy. A language does not cease to live because it ceases to be spoken.

(7.) In studying Latin we are taking possession of the key of the Romance languages, shortening the time needed for acquiring these by at least one-half.

(8.) The study of Latin introduces the pupil in its later stages to a conscious discernment of Art in language—the artistic or beautiful in expression. And this to a degree which no modern tongue can do, because, first, of its chaste severity of form; and secondly, because being so far removed from our own time we can look at it as a fresh and alien object. Thus, by contrast, our implicit feelings regarding literary form in our own tongue are brought into explicit consciousness—raised, in short, from mere feeling into knowledge.

(9.) The study of Latin, as a dead tongue, especially in its later stages, when it is accompanied by the study of the life, art, and literature of Rome, has a remarkable influence on the tone of thought and character. It has this influence by connecting us in a living way with what seems, but truly is not, a dead past, and thereby expanding our intellectual and moral sympathies so as to embrace that past as part of our own life. It makes us members of a larger human society. Modern cotemporary language and life are too near to our own to have this cultivating influence to the same extent, and do not teach us to see things in a true perspective; they may be said to broaden our lives, but they do not lengthen them. Neither the Hindu nor the Chinese language and life would serve, because these are not *our* past. The ancient life, by thus stimulating the historical imagination and carrying it out of the present, tends to give balance of mind, checks sciolism of opinion and crudeness of judgment, based on a narrow induction of things which, as being close at hand, are apt to assume undue importance. The true humanity of the growing boy is thus deepened and strengthened.

I do not here speak of the larger culture which Latin, as literature and as the embodiment of the attitude of the Roman mind to life and social polity, gives to the university scholar who has mastered these. The education of the people is not to be regulated in the interest of either literary or linguistic or historical experts. We have to think of boys and the school only. All else can take care of itself.

It might be said, and has been said by certain arid utilitarians, that the study of the history of Rome and the reading of translations would do much that I attribute to the study of the language of Rome. But this is a mistake. By the perusal of the history, and by the study of translations, much could be done doubtless; but the result would fall far short of our aims. The true history of a country is the thought and literature and art of that country; and I know very little of any people if I know it merely in its annals of events, even if I also exhibit in bold and effective relief its great characters (which is not always done). I *know* a people only by living contact of mind with mind, of humanity with humanity, and this is alone possible by contact with its language and literature. This is to know its true history, its true significance as a factor in the world's progress, because this alone is to know its inner life by ourselves living with it. If we may regard "Culture" as marking the universal, as opposed to the national and parochial, element in the educated mind, it will be found, if genuine and not spurious, to have its roots in historical sympathy.

The reasons for the study of Latin which have been given might be very much amplified and elaborated; but I am not here defending against opponents the importance of this special kind of linguistic instruction. My sole object is, by bringing before you the reasons *why* we learn Latin, to introduce you, in a rational way, to the question *how* we should teach and learn Latin. Each one of the reasons which I have above assigned has a direct bearing on method, because method is a way, a road to certain ends. Think, then, of these ends, and try to inquire the road to them for yourselves, and you will, so far as these ends at least are concerned, have constructed for yourselves a method of teaching Latin.

It will be observed that I have not included among the reasons for teaching Latin the reading of the Latin classics in after-life. I am speaking of the education of the secondary school, not of the rare results of university study. The "far-off interest of years" can never be realised even by those boys who spend eight or nine years on Latin and Greek; even university fellows are not understood to find their nightly recreation in Æschylus when they leave the common room. Just as little would I be disposed to try to make you believe at this time of day that Latin and Greek are synonymous with a liberal education. On the contrary, a man of exclusive classical training is illiberally educated, so illiberally educated that he does not even know it. The cause of the ancient tongues is lost if we rest it on untenable grounds. Nor would I urge as an argument that classical men can alone write English. This is contrary to fact. They are generally poor writers of English, and that just in proportion to their devotion to the ancient classics. There is, however, a certain wholesome severity of intellect about classically trained men in their treatment of all subjects, whereas in the scientific man we find this only in strictly scientific subjects. This result is a great gain; but it is just possible that it might be generated by **an** equally thorough **training in** English, French, and German. **There is little opportunity** of trying the experiment; **for young men** who wish **to** combine intellectual **work with** cash-**rewards must** take **to** the paying subjects — Greek and Latin. In any case we know from experience the great formative power of Latin.

This is **not an** essay on classical education. **Were** I to criticise, **in** a hostile **spirit,** the claims of classical **and** humanistic education, **my** first objection **to it** would be that in **the** school **the** boasted education is not classical, and not humanistic; and **my** second would be that it is anti-Hellenic. **We do** not attain the Greek attitude, **of** mind **by** dissecting Greek, any **more** than we attain **to** the **spirit of** Christ by virtue **of** our knowledge of **New** Testament philology. Do you imagine, for **a moment, that if the** Athenians had discovered **Sanskrit, they** would have **trained** their **boys on the** Vedic **hymns and** the Mahabhârâta? Can you think of a Pericles or a **Plato burying** the nine Muses out of sight, and carefully eschewing music, art, national literature, and history, and guarding their boys from such frivolous society by involving them **in** Sanskrit and Zend and *putting all the money on these?*[1] In the *manner* **of** our devotion **to** Latin **and** Greek **we are** conspicuously un-Greek. **To** have a frank **open eye for** all **that is**

---

[1] This expression has been ignorantly **objected to. It** is surely well known that **in** Great Britain **the surest way to** the *material rewards* of the universities is by distinction in Latin and Greek.

beautiful, to give a hospitable reception to all that presents itself as knowledge, to train in past heroisms and in present civic duties, this is to be Hellenic. The Athenian gave boys material which nourished and enlarged the mind. But I forego these polemical temptations and turn to my immediate subject, the method of teaching Latin.

LECTURE X.

METHOD OF TEACHING LATIN.

In teaching Latin we have to keep the reasons for teaching it always in mind. They yield rules and directions for procedure which, to a considerable extent, are peculiar to the teaching of Latin. But we have also to keep in mind that the majority of our pupils must leave us for the business of life before they have acquired, even fairly well, the language or languages we teach them. Consequently, the rule which is applicable to every subject is specially applicable here—viz. that our *method be such as to give to every pupil the full benefit of the training and discipline which the language is presumed to afford and which the pupil's age admits of, at whatever point he may cease to study it.* Herein lies one of the claims which all method permanently makes on the teacher—that it secures this admirable result. Each day's lesson justifies itself.

It has been often said of late, that it is useless to teach boys Latin if they cannot look forward to a prolonged curriculum. My experience leads me to dissent from this emphatically. In three years Latin, *well-taught*, and not begun prematurely, can give an amount of genuine discipline and solid instruction in words and syntax forms which is invaluable. It places a boy, as it were, by one bound on a higher intellectual plane than his fellows.

Those of you who remember the first lecture of this course, will see that the functions of Language as an instrument of education, as giving food and training, as giving discipline, and as giving cultivation of the æsthetic perceptions, are all included in the reasons assigned for teaching Latin; and, in due degree, any other foreign tongue.

I might here introduce all the rules of method as deduced from the facts of psychology,[1] and apply them to the teaching of Latin. I content myself with the more important.

1. *Teach one thing on the basis of another which is already known; for the mind advances to new knowledge on the basis of what it already knows. Knowledge is an organic growth, not a mechanical one.*

The old knowledge out of which the new language must grow is the knowledge of the vernacular.

As regards vocables, this is clear enough. *Musa* and *dominus* have no meaning to anybody except in so far as a "song" or "muse," or a "lord," are already known. We must know the "thing," whatever it may be, in our own tongue, before we seek to know it in another.

[1] See *Institutes of Education*.

If the new is to grow out of the old, **Latin grammar,** no less than Latin **vocables,** ought to grow out of English grammar. A boy should be able **to parse** fairly well, and be familiar with the relations of clauses in English sentences, before he begins Latin.

A certain type of classical teacher, now nearly **outworn, tell us,** "There is no English grammar, properly speaking;" "**Boys** never learn English grammar thoroughly till they know Latin grammar;" "Boys, in fact, **cannot do it.**" **In brief,** English grammar is Latin **grammar; for I** suppose that is what it all amounts **to.** Even to deny this **is** now, I hope, an anachronism. That the boy who **knows** German will thereby **know** English grammar better than the boy who does not know German, is **true;** still more certain **is it** that the boy who knows Latin will know English grammar better than the boy **who does** not know **Latin.** Everybody will **admit this;** but it **is** an absurd inference that **the** knowledge of English grammar *depends* on a knowledge of German or Latin. **All** that it means at bottom is, **to use the** words of Goethe, "A man who knows *only* his own language does not know even that."

Enough on this **point.** Let us stand by the rule:— The **new should grow out of** the old. A boy, therefore, should not be introduced to Latin at all until he has a firm hold **of English** accidence, parsing, and general analysis. We should find **boys** in this way make much more rapid, certainly **surer,** and always **more** intelligent, progress with Latin. What they did **would have** meaning and **interest.**

In connection with this, let me say that the arrangement of tenses and moods in the conjugation of English verbs should, as much as possible, correspond with that adopted in the Latin grammar. Latin might, perhaps, meet the English here half-way; for example, the subjunctive mood might be called "Potential *and* Subjunctive." In this way it would be seen clearly that it was used both for the English Potential, "I may be," and the English Subjunctive, "If I be;" and so forth.[1]

In syntax a good deal more in the way of preparing for Latin can be done than is generally admitted. Thorough English parsing, in which the relations of the predicative verb to subject and object, etc., are fully brought out, would do very much to promote a clearer and quicker comprehension of Latin syntax as being not something altogether alien to English, but only different. Remember, too, that if we forfeit the discipline obtained by contrasting English and Latin, we imperil the teaching of Latin altogether, for we thus abolish one of its chief uses for boys.

It follows from what has been said, that quite the earliest age for beginning Latin should be the second year of the upper-primary period, viz. the thirteenth year, save in exceptional cases.

2. *The real, or concrete, should precede the abstract,* as

---

[1] Parallel Grammars recently published by Sonnenschein & Co. try to give effect to this idea. They are very instructive, and are well spoken of.

this order accords with **the natural growth and operation of mind.**

As regards vocables, for example; a certain number of these should be supplied in connection with every declension and conjugation as the paradigm of each is acquired; but they should, in the first instance, be restricted to things of sense; *e.g.* the names of the more common animals should be given, and in connection with these, the parts of the animal. You give *taurus* and *vacca*; give next *cornu, pes, os, cauda,* and so forth. Then bring in those adjectives which are fitly and usually applied to these things, viz. forms, colours, etc. Thereby also you fulfil a further rule of method which requires that you "associate teachings." A boy will remember with ease all the Latin words you can use in speaking of a cow, if you have a picture of a cow before him and keep to its external characters. No Latin words should be given in the earliest stages, except those which denote things already familiar. Do not be afraid of interesting your boys too much in their work.

3. "*Teach generalisations as generalisations.*"

That is to say, we must base all generalisation on the particular and concrete, which alone gives the general and abstract any meaning. Rules of syntax are generalisations, and they are to be constructed out of the initiatory reading lessons by the pupil with the help of the master. As the pupil gradually acquires them, he will write them down as formulated for him by the teacher on the blackboard, and enter them at home in a grammar note-book. Here again the association with concrete instances helps the memory. And still again (for all sound rules of method help each other), you evoke the will of the pupil, and by giving him a sense of power in construction, you elicit intellectual interest.

It is said that if the boys are told to learn the generalisations by heart at once, and apply them as occasion arises, they will learn them sooner. But this old-fashioned notion is simply not true. Very few ever learn them at all so as to see their true bearing on the concrete. By the inductive method they *must* see this; their memory, also, as I have said, is helped by the rationality of the connection and by association with particulars, and they thus cannot help learning *more quickly*. Besides, quickness of acquisition is not everything: the course of instruction must be *solid* and *sure*, as well as quick.

Then there is the question of intellectual training and discipline, one of our chief reasons for teaching Latin at all. The inductive method gives these in addition to all its other advantages. Is it to be supposed that the method of teaching any subject which is the most educative, is the most ineffective? This would be a strange contradiction in nature. Let the teacher always remember that he is teaching a *mind*, and not this or that subject *to* a mind. I would repeat here what I said in speaking of English grammar: it is by constant examples met with in reading, not by rule or precept or laboured exposition, that boys realise the generalisations of grammar.

It is not, of course, meant that a boy is to wait till he sees a very large number of "instances" before he completes his induction. He is not a grammatical investigator, save in a boy sense. The rules of the art of education provide for this as well as for other things. The boy, if his will is to be evoked, must be self-instructing; but the teacher is to be his "guide and co-operator," and so lead him to a result which, left to himself alone, he would never reach. This is what teaching means.

When Latin is properly taught, every lesson is an inductive investigation: every translation, if taught in the same spirit, is a fresh problem demanding the analytico-synthetic operation of intellect.

4. *Turn to Use.*

We never truly know even a word or form, much less a linguistic rule, until we have used them. "By playing on the lyre we become lyre-players," says Aristotle. Every acquisition in the shape of words or generalisations, accordingly, must be turned to use, *from the very beginning,* for the making of Latin. No lesson in Latin is a complete lesson which does not embrace this. Oral composition, and composition by the help of the blackboard, must be a part of every lesson from the first. Give the boy *est* and *sunt* and *non,* and you can begin before the end of the first week. Masters, who wisely do this, are yet apt to trust too much to books. Now books, especially good ones, are very useful in their own way and place. But teachers will never understand teaching till they learn to regard books as merely subsidiary, and as necessary evils. No man certainly has a right to teach any subject whatsoever until he is independent of books. It must all be *in him*. He must be saturated with his subject. Such teaching as I refer to is more laborious for the teacher, and, as a matter of course, we have his indolence finding arguments against it. One thing is certain, that such teaching attains its end; that the other way, which, under more or less of disguise, is the rote-way, has utterly failed, requires no evidence. *Circumspice.* Prize pigs from Belfast are unsatisfactory evidence that all, or even the majority of, the pigs in Ireland take on fat. So with a few university scholarship hunters: what of all the other boys? See Reports of Commissions.

The boy, remember, has learnt, or is daily learning, the more common Latin vocables, under each declension and conjugation, which have reference to things of the *sensible world and of ordinary life*, and these can at once be utilised. The making of Latin will advance with the growing knowledge and growing intelligence of the boy, just as English does or ought to do. All the vocables acquired should be turned to use by being thrown into living connection one with another, and not be left in columnar isolation. If our aim were simply to fit boys to make acquaintance with

Latin literature in the original, it would, perhaps, be difficult to maintain the imperativeness of this early necessity of Latin composition; but this is not our sole, or even our chief, aim. Even professed scholars do not, as a rule, read Latin literature, after they have graduated, except as business. These early exercises should be oral in the first instance, and embrace gradually some of the common concerns of life. If a proper selection of vocables to be learned by heart is given (in accordance with Rule 2), and if a few verbs are early thrown in, this practice of oral composition is quite feasible. Only simple sentences are to be attempted, to begin with. In training to synthetic and imitative composition in the vernacular, I pointed out the importance of requiring the boy to answer questions in complete sentences, and this rule might, perhaps, be attended to in Latin also with advantage. Let me add: teach nothing in the grammar that is useless. It is a mistake to suppose that a thing is of educational importance in proportion to its remoteness from "use."

5. *Present to Sense.*—*The eye should be appealed to whenever practicable.*

One is almost ashamed to go on quoting Horace's "Segnius irritant," etc. (A. P. 180).

Strange that men should have been so slow in applying a precept so obvious. A Latin class without the use of a blackboard, on which every new word and sentence and rule may be written distinctly, is an anachronism. You have not taught anything capable of being presented to the *eye* until you have taught it *through* the eye, as well as through the ear. Were it possible to smell it and taste it and touch it, you should also teach it through the nose, the mouth, and the skin. The senses thus establish their own associations, and aid memory.

Before leaving this rule of method, I would, by way of subsidiary suggestion, say that it would be well were the Latin declensions and conjugations exhibited in black letters on wall-maps, so as to catch the eye, and taught in school from these maps, *after they have been first constructively worked out on the blackboard* by the boys under the master's guidance. In exercising the boys in elementary composition, oral or written, and in parsing, an indication of any error made, by simply pointing with the rod to such a wall-map, would be very efficacious. The correction of the error would be thus associated with locality, and with the eye, as well as the ear.

In reading Cæsar, or any other historian, graphic maps of the country should be constantly present and constantly referred to. In battles, the master should draw on the blackboard the position of the opposing forces. In other reading, antiquities should be represented by drawings and photographs wherever possible —not by words.

In conclusion, nothing *new* should be taught which is not presented to the eye on the board. How short-sighted is it of a master to give for the first time *scindo,* and merely *tell* the conjugation of it; and yet how universal the practice!

6. *Step by step: step after step.* The teacher of Latin should set down in his school diary (which should be a kind of appendix to his Instruction-plan of the school) the curriculum through which he means to carry the boy, and the definite amount to be taught in successive months, terms, and years. Little, and that little well, should be his motto. Any other mode of procedure is loose and vague, and there is a want of genuine earnestness about it.

7. *Evoke the Will.*

In order that any subject of instruction, or any part of a subject, may be really grasped, the boy must bring his own will to bear on it, with a view to apprehension and comprehension. He must not sit passively and have things placed before him by his teacher. You have to pump out of him, not to pump into him. The teacher is the caterer, guide, and co-operator; but that is all. His duty is simply to direct the pupil what to do in due order and succession, and to get the pupil to do it. Apply this to the getting-up of prescribed lessons:—

The master having, after due thought as the guide of his pupil, "set the lesson," the boys should be required to attack it in the schoolroom under his guidance. The present practice of converting schools into repetition halls, where the work done elsewhere is merely "said over," the master relieving himself of all true effort to educate, and indeed even to instruct, by letting boys pit themselves one against another for places, while he merely keeps the game going, is not education—not even instruction. The true work is done elsewhere, if it is done at all. As caterer and co-operator, I say, the master should put the next lesson before the boys, and, supposing it be a new declension or conjugation, get the boys to follow him as he writes it down on the board, requiring them to *find out for themselves*, and to point out, its resemblances to, and differences from, what has been already acquired. Those resemblances and differences being thus worked out, should be written down in bold characters by the master on the board. A few minutes spent asking questions on what is thus written down, secures that instruction in the lesson has been given—and how? By the boys to themselves — with the co-operation of the master, and organically because the new is learned through similarity and difference with the old. The boys have had an intellectual exercise, and the result is intelligent perception. This, observe, is discipline so far as it goes, and if the boy left school for good that very day, he would yet carry with him something better than knowledge. It is *only now*, after the above process, that memory comes into requisition; and the boy should be expected to prepare overnight nothing save what has been first done and understood in the school.

So with translation: the master, having heard a few read the lesson of the previous day and having done the parsing carefully (or as much of it as there is time for), should state generally the substance of the next chapter, and turn the boys on to the learning of it under his guidance and co-operation—sentence by sentence. After a pause, he calls for translation, and if there be considerable difficulties, he points out the leading clause of the sentence, and gives such other limited assistance as he considers necessary. The passage being thus worked out in co-operation, the master should then require the boys to bring a written translation on the following day. While the other boys look on, this written translation should be read by one or two of the cleverer boys, who might then collect the other exercises and correct them. This being done—and it ought not to take more than fifteen minutes—there should be oral construing of the passage. The teacher should then make the boys parse one sentence in full detail, repeating, word for word, every rule hitherto learned, confining himself in this exercise to the worse half of his class. The *verbs* of the rest of the lesson having been conjugated, he will proceed to the preparation of the next lesson, in co-operation with his pupils.

By thus making out the lesson along with the master, with a view to the working of it out by himself at night with the help of a dictionary, the boy more truly does his share in the learning than by the present plan, according to which a few boys prepare their work independently, but the great majority are dependent either on tutors or on cribs, or on copying down the master's reading of the next lesson (which, of course, is a crib), or on their neighbours.

If you do not think the above a good plan, and are of opinion that boys really instruct themselves best by getting their lessons to prepare without any previous assistance, and by using the school simply as a repetition and testing place, you will at least see the importance of causing the boy to write out his translations daily. By so doing he cannot shirk his work: he truly must apply his mind to the bit of Latin before him in order to reproduce it in written language; and so far he instructs himself. You may say, How can I know in that case that a boy instructs himself? He may have a tutor, or use a crib, in his own home. To which the answer is: For the former you are not responsible, and the latter you can find out with perfect ease. You test him by the oral construing which follows the reading of the written translations, and, further, you have simply occasionally to require the written exercise to be done in the school under your own eye. In any case a test will be applied at your regular written class examinations, which should be fortnightly. Masters talk against cribs, but if they do not purposely wink at the use of them, they are at least indifferent about it. It is very easy for them to detect the practice, if they choose to try. So much for daily written translations, which should be clearly and carefully done. If you think the lesson too long to be written out, you can give the most important part of it.

Consider, further, the bearing of this practice on another of our reasons for teaching Latin—its utility in giving a comprehension of English. These written translations are English composition exercises of the very best kind, because they are regulated, as to their *form*, by a language whose syntactical construction is close and logical, and because the matter of the composition is supplied, as it ought to be.

Finally, with a view to instruction in shades of meaning and exact and literary reproduction, as distinguished from close construing, you should conclude the lesson by reading a translation made by yourself in your best style, taking advantage of the best cribs in doing this.

8. "*Be exact and thorough,*" *for all knowledge as it is acquired must be exact, if it is to afford a sound basis for further organic building-up of the subject in the mind of the pupil.*

Note the importance of this, not only as making progress possible, but in view of one of our reasons for teaching Latin—that it is a formal *discipline* of intellect. How can there be any *discipline* where there is no exactness and thoroughness? This is all-important. And yet how loosely Latin is taught! That lax translation which boys make in a class, trusting to some sudden inspiration, or to a prompter, or to the master, is a training in inexactness, and is positively hurtful both to the intelligence and the moral nature of a boy. With a view to exactness, observe again the advantages of much writing. A boy in writing out his lesson ascertains his own ignorance: in oral work he never knows (save in a few exceptional cases) whether he has accomplished his task or not.

This habit of writing also, let me add, gives a sense of power and progress, and of independent activity. Thus it is that one good rule of method supports every other rule, and is supported by them in turn. Observe again, for example, how this rule of writing out with a view to exactness gives effect to the rule, "Present to Sense." In the written exercise, the boy creates for himself a thing to look at, and does it with an intentness and application which insures its being retained: for he recognises his Latin through a fresh sense (as it were)—the sense of *touch* in the manual act of writing. Still once more, note how a sound rule of method tells in every direction: the habit of writing extends the number of associations with the work done, and so helps the memory.

Exactness in the knowledge of the day's translation means that no boy shall leave it till he thoroughly knows it. The thorough "lessoning" (to use Milton's word) of one book is, to my mind, as essential to sound progress as it is to discipline.

9. *Confine your teaching to the leading outlines or salient facts in the first instance, and gradually fill in details.*

This rule is based on the psychological fact that *thus* we perceive and conceive.

In Latin syntax, then, confine yourself to a few rules at first, until they are sufficiently understood, and then go on to others. The rules should be grammatical, not logical. The boy has his own grammar note-book, and enters them as they occur.

If this requirement of method apply to the ordinary rules of syntax, how much more does it apply to idioms, and exceptions, and irregularities! And yet the old practice (old, though not yet antiquated) was to cram them all down together. With what result?

10. Again I recur to the all-important rule, TURN TO USE: this time in connection with more advanced work—the translation lesson of the day.

You have read a chapter of Nepos, or of Cæsar, having prepared it in the manner explained above. You have parsed all the verbs, and also such portion of the lesson *in extreme detail* as there is time for. But you have not yet done with the chapter. What is the significance of the chapter in view of the reasons for teaching Latin, and the acquisition of the Latin tongue? It is clear to me that you have not *used* the chapter until you have extracted from it (1) all the vocables, (2) all the syntax, (3) all the making of Latin, (4) all the English, which it will yield.

(1.) *Vocables:* I do not mean to say that you are to build up on the foundation of the words occurring in the lesson *all* their derivatives, but that you are to build up all the *more commonly used* cognates and derivatives. It is extraordinary what a mass of vocables the first book of Cæsar's "Gallic War" will thus yield. These groups of cognates the boy will enter either at the end of his grammar note-book, or in a separate book.

(2.) So we proceed with syntax. The lesson must deliver up to the boy *all* the syntax he has as yet learned, and extend his knowledge.

(3.) So also we proceed with the making of Latin. To-day we make Latin out of yesterday's chapter, in a free and varied way. No exercise in Latin composition excites the interest or supplies the discipline which retroversion of the English of past chapters into Latin does. On this, indeed, we mainly rely for Latin composition, using composition books as mere accessories and helps.

(4.) The English that lies *in* the Latin has to be taught. For great numbers of English words are only now revealed to the pupil in their origins and primary significance; and thus one of the chief reasons for our teaching Latin is satisfied.

I am well aware that some boys will be left behind, however good the teaching; but they will learn something at least, and they will be disciplined, both intellectually and morally, by the thoroughness and honesty of the work. I am also well aware that there may not be always time to exhaust every lesson. But have the right mode of procedure as your aim: this is the essential thing.

A single chapter of Cæsar thus thoroughly and exactly *known*, or "lessoned," is worth twenty loosely, or even fairly, gone over. As a *discipline* you will at once admit that this is so. But besides, as I have already pointed out, every rule of sound method helps the others, and the (so-called) *practical* outcome is also thus best secured. With such thoroughness and exactness as I demand, a boy would take a considerable time to get over the fifty-four chapters of Lib. I. of, say, the "Gallic War." He would study only twelve chapters per month; but are five months, or even six months, too much to devote to the first book of Cæsar, if at the end of that time a boy truly knows it, and has constructed his own note-books out of it? He will have learned more, quite apart from discipline, than by four books read as they are too commonly read. To Latin, as to other studies, the rule of Quintilian is applicable: "Cito scribendo non fit ut bene scribatur, bene scribendo fit ut cito" (x. 3. 9).

(5.) Finally, you turn to use the knowledge the boys have attained, by setting them down to write out translations of "unseen" passages once a week.

11. *Exercise the Memory. Revise.*

All the above rules make remembrance easy, for they presume understanding, they involve closeness of application, and they give free play to association. But all this is insufficient: there must be constant revision if boys are to remember what they have acquired. What a grown man will remember after one telling, has to be told twenty times to a boy. A day once a week should be set apart for revisal, and a "grand" day once a month. When the pupil begins Latin poetry, prescribe the learning by heart of lines. Not too many. A few, well-learned—this is all that is needed.

Some would teach the accidence bit by bit, as it is artificially introduced in a series of exercises, and so postpone the daily reading of an author. They seem to have a superstitious fear of calling on a boy to learn by heart. The pupil should, of course, be intelligently introduced to the accidence, declensions and conjugations being compared, and the stems of words being emphasised; but when this has been done he should be required to learn them off by heart, and to give the Latin for the English almost as if he were an automatic machine. If this is drudgery, then let him drudge: we all have to drudge; but it seems to me that boys rather like it. "Aussi longtemps," says M. Bréal,[1] "qu'on fera du Latin, il faudra décliner des noms, conjuguer des verbes, apprendre des règles de formation : l'important est de le faire avec intelligence."

12. *Associate Teachings.* Vocables in the earliest stage are associated with things or images of things, and, with as little delay as possible, *with other words* in a sentence. The sentence must be the unit of the language to the pupil. You associate also every new

[1] *De l'enseignement des Langues Anciennes.*

teaching with a previous teaching, getting the pupil to point out the likeness of the new to the old. This connects itself with Rule 1. You associate also the Latin with the English.

What has now to be said concerns the middle of the third year and thereafter.

13. I would now touch on the ninth reason for learning Latin, and deduce this rule: *A pupil must be so instructed that he shall attain a grasp of the sweep, characteristics, and genius of the language, and a general acquaintance with the literature and history of the Roman people.*

In the earlier stages of study, little can be done in this direction, it is true. More, however, than is generally supposed may be accomplished. The slow, exact, and critical way in which the regular Latin lesson should be done may possibly weary boys. To obviate this, and to give your pupils relief and some acquaintance with Latin literature, and a larger comprehension of the sweep and character and capacity of the language than they can otherwise get, there ought to be *cursive* reading in every class above the second. For example, while engaged closely and critically on the first book of Cæsar, the master might read *with the boys* some such book as Eutropius or Cornelius Nepos—translating a sentence, calling on some one to do it after him, and then hurrying on to the next sentence. In this way the whole of Eutropius and the Latin lives in Cornelius Nepos might be read during the year in which the boys are working critically at Cæsar and Ovid. In the following year, when the boys are engaged on Sallust and Virgil, or some of the simpler orations of Cicero, all the more interesting portions of the eight books of the "Gallic War" might be cursively read—the substance of those portions omitted being narrated by the master. While Livy, again, is being *studied*, Curtius's "Life of Alexander the Great" might be read in the same way. While Horace is being critically and exactly studied, much of Ovid might be cursively read. I would also encourage, for cursive and private reading, editions with the Latin on one side and the English on the other. In short, every means should be taken to make the boy familiar with a large *mass* of the language and literature which he is studying.

It is scarcely necessary to say under this rule, that when a new book, say the twenty-second book of Livy, or a book of Tacitus, is begun, it is necessary to give wholeness and fulness and unity to a boy's conceptions, if you are to engage his rational interest. Therefore, give him an account (with a good map before him) of the history of Rome or Greece, dwelling on the great events that happened prior to the date at which they begin to read. Let them know also about Livy and Tacitus, and lead them to take a living interest in their writings, not as so many word-puzzles constructed two thousand years ago for schoolboys, with a view to determine who is to be head boy of a class on a certain day in the nineteenth century. Ample introductions, more than once repeated, to the books read critically, will be the certain means of interesting boys, if anything will, in the Latin language through its literature and history. For the teacher, too, it is valuable: it connects him through the humanities with the hearts and intellects of his pupils, and helps to establish his moral influence. If Latin be not taught in this large spirit, even that admirable tongue, with all its great educative advantages, will not permanently hold its own against the intrusion of science-teaching accompanied by modern languages.

By the end of the fourth year, your boys, if taught in accordance with the above suggestions, will have read, with much more exactness and thoroughness than is now common, all the usual material, they will have written or spoken a hundred Latin translations and Latin prose exercises for one now written, have thoroughly worked out the English relations of the Latin tongue, and in the course of doing all this have constructed their own syntactical grammar and idiom book: nay, over and above, they will have read cursively, or with the help of translations, the whole of Eutropius, of Cornelius Nepos, of Cæsar's "Gallic War" (the passages omitted being orally narrated), and all the more interesting legends of Ovid's "Metamorphoses;" and although they may have read only one book of the "Æneid" critically, you, the master, will have found time to read to them the whole of some good poetical translation. Compare this with the miserable scraps and disconnected fragments which at present constitute the Latin diet of boys. And yet the men who from day to day give these scraps and word-puzzles tell you that they do so in the name of the Humanities.

You see, then, that while I advocate much more verbal thoroughness and much more Latin composition than is at present practised, in the interest at once of discipline and acquisition, I also advocate much more looseness and breadth. The mode of procedure suggested is more intensive, and at the same time more extensive. It is scarcely necessary to point out how the exact and critical, as well as more extensive, reading of Latin gives opportunities for complying with the requirements involved in our third reason for studying Latin—the analysis of the shades of meaning between words, and the finer turns of linguistic expression.

Doubtless those of you who have already taught Latin will say that the carrying out of this system of constant writing, and of Latin composition, would be extremely difficult with a class exceeding thirty-five, or composed of boys at different stages of progress. To which the answer is, that classes should not be composed of more than thirty-five, and that they should not be at different stages of progress. Indeed, no class should be larger than thirty.

If all this can be done to introduce boys into the life and spirit and genius of the Roman people, by the end of their fourth year in Latin, presuming that they begin in their twelfth or thirteenth year, I need scarcely say that much more is to be expected when the study of Latin is prolonged two years beyond this.

The exercises in the making of Latin should now be more varied. Retroversion should still be practised, but the boys should also be required to reproduce the *substance* of several chapters of the Latin author they are reading; and to prevent too much reliance on the book, these exercises should be done as much as possible in school.

By following the procedure above detailed, we associate the study of a language with the realities and humanities of which all literary language is the vehicle, and bring ourselves into accord with our eighth as well as our ninth reason for teaching Latin. In continuing our course of instruction further, we follow the same method, and are led into a still higher sphere of the humanities, encountering our eighth reason for teaching Latin, which yields us a rule of method, as the other reasons do: viz.

14. *So instruct in more advanced Latin as to cultivate the æsthetic and art perceptions of your pupils.*

You read Horace and Virgil and Livy, we may assume, and require written translations, if not of the whole lesson read, of a part of it, and you maintain your daily exercises in Latin composition, oral and written, on the basis of the passages read. You also continue your cursive reading, and encourage the boys to continue it at home with the help of translations. But this is not enough. When you have read an eloquent passage in Cicero, or a fine passage in Virgil or Horace, you should ask your boys to note its eloquence or its beauty. Their attention should be directed to the art with which the thought is expressed. To define literary art with exactness is impossible; but, in any case, we are safe in saying that it is the adequate expression of an idea—neither more nor less than adequate—in language worthy of the idea and controlled by the feeling of the beautiful. And the beautiful, whatever else it may be, is severe, is chaste, is self-controlled, balanced, like a Greek statue; and it is all this because it is simplicity and harmony. State the idea in your own words, or ask your pupils to do it in their words, and then point out how nobly, and yet with what chaste simplicity or eloquent rhythm, the orator or poet has given expression to what in our limited utterance is mean enough. The boys should continue, of course, to learn the finer pieces of poetry by heart.

Then, when you have read a piece of Horace or Virgil, pronounce to them, with fit elocution, the best poetical translations in our own tongue. Dryden, Conington, Martin, will, as a matter of course, be in the library and schoolroom of every classical teacher. I am almost disposed to say that no boy ever became fully aware *for the first time* of the beauty, the (so-called) "classical" flavour, of any piece of Latin or Greek except through a good translation. If he is an expert, he may doubtless by the time he is five-and-twenty make this for himself; but we are speaking of schools and 999 out of a thousand Latin and Greek pupils. If you want a boy of seventeen or eighteen to feel the *Greek* of the Hippolytus, for example, he must read with you Fitzgerald's translation. He will certainly not discover it by the help of the dictionary. It is at this stage, also, that parallel passages are in place.

In home exercises, *elegant* English renderings will now be encouraged, and much, very much, educational value attached to them.

Do not forget at this stage to deepen and broaden the pupil's knowledge of the history and life of Rome. Every lesson in Latin is a starting-point for all that it suggests of Roman life and civilisation. Read to him translations of the best passages in the Livian History; present to his eyes maps of the geography of the ancient world; exhibit photographs of Rome, of its great buildings, of its works of art. The room should be adorned with casts from the British Museum. The whole atmosphere should be classical. Remember, too, that in the most brilliant period of Roman literature with which you are now dealing, it was Greece which was the mother of Roman arts. You are now on Grecian soil, and as boys have by this time begun Greek and made some way in it, you can improve on the Roman lesson.

A boy who, after six years in Latin begun at the age of about twelve, to which he has given an average of eight school hours per week, has not read, either in the original tongue (critically or cursively), or with the help of translations, the whole of Cæsar's "Gallic War," Cornelius Nepos, Sallust, Virgil, Horace, seven or eight orations of Cicero, all the best books of Livy, all Tacitus, all that is best in the "Tristia," "Epistolæ ex Ponto," and "Metamorphoses" of Ovid, two or three plays of Plautus and Terence, and selections from Catullus, Tibullus, Martial, and Lucretius, has failed to get the full benefit of a Latin course. And need I add that the master who is incompetent to extract from Latin study all its historical teaching and all its æsthetic and moral culture, as well as its logical discipline, is not a true builder of the Temple of Education, but a mere hodman—a carrier of bricks and mortar, out of which others are to rear the stately and beautiful edifice, if it is to be reared at all?

The application of any one of the above rules of method will touch the intelligence and evoke the interest of boys: much more all of them taken together. Do not be afraid to see your boys happy and interested in their work. There is absolutely no reason in the nature of things why the schoolroom should be regarded by a boy as part of "that estate of sin and misery whereinto men fell" through Adam.

NOTE.—As to Latin verse-writing, I presume that as an universally prescribed exercise, and consequent engine of immorality, it is now gone out. But I cannot agree with those who wholly condemn it. For the highest stages of progress, for which alone, like elegant prose, it is suited, it does much, if pursued in moderation, to enable a youth to realise the genius of the ancients and to appreciate literary form. And whenever boys spend more than four years at Latin, I think nonsense verses and the retroversion of translations from Latin poets a valuable as well as interesting exercise.

Greek.

I might now go on to deal with Greek, but, if I did so, I should simply have to repeat what I have said about Latin. The only warning to be given is, that the "old" out of which Greek instruction grows is Latin. To bother boys, for example, with Greek syntax rules which are the same as those in Latin, is superfluous. It is differences and contrasts the teacher has now to bring to view. This is an essential part of the discipline which language gives, as well as the best way of instructing.

It seems to me that Epic and Ionic dialects should not be touched by the boy (still less learned in the grammar) until an Attic foundation has been securely laid. By that time the great mass of the boys will be gone from school. Why teach Greek at all to boys who cannot prosecute it beyond Anab. B. I.? There is much that might be more advantageously taught. One would think that many classical masters regard with an almost fanatical hostility English, French, German, Physical Geography, Elementary Science, and History. If Greek be taught, it is surely reasonable to expect that boys of seventeen, who leave school without proceeding to the university, should have a good knowledge of Greek history, have read Plutarch's "Lives" in English, the whole of the "Iliad" and "Odyssey" in the original (large portions cursively, others critically), the whole of the "Anabasis," a portion of Arrian, the whole of Herodotus in English if not in Greek (this writer being used to lay the foundations of ancient universal history), two or three Greek dramas in the original, and most of the others in translations. Without this breadth of treatment Greek cannot long keep hold of our secondary schools. The instruction and discipline which stop at Grammar can be obtained without the heavy burden of Greek. Only for the few who go forward for classical honours at our universities could the retention of Greek be justified, if it be not taken up in this large and humanistic sense.

LECTURE XI.

METHOD OF TEACHING MODERN LANGUAGES—FRENCH.

IF French or German is to be seriously taught, the *minimum* allowance of school time should be five hours a week.

In teaching modern languages, the rules of method are the same as in English and Latin. As we are dealing with living speech, the ear must be constantly exercised independently of the eye; and what in Latin is oral composition, takes the form of Conversation—based chiefly on the daily lessons. Here too, as in Latin and Greek, much cursive reading should be done. Nor is there any reason why, at the proper age, Molière and other writers should not be read to the pupils in English as a foretaste of the French.

It has been suggested to me that the rules of method should be applied to the teaching of French; and, consequently, in this second edition, I shall endeavour to give their application in outline, but not in detail. Teachers who are dependent on detail laid down by another will not be successful.

Rule 1 (p. 134). This means that English grammar

must be known before French is begun. But it does not mean that no French vocables or conversational phrases are to be learned before English Grammar is known, care being taken of the pronunciation at this imitative stage of language-instruction.

Rule 2. The vocables learned should be the names of things of sense—the first which a child learns in his own language. The process is simply a repetition of the first stage of *object-lessons* in French instead of English. You point to an object or a picture, and give the French name for it. Always prefix the article, *e.g. the* horse *le* (or *un*) *cheval, the* woman *la* (or *une*) *femme.* The memory associates the word with *the thing seen*, as well with the English equivalent. Thus the greater number of the nouns of child conversation, *e.g.* of the parts of the body, clothes, animals, etc., may be acquired easily and *pleasantly.* Having done this, then repeat these exercises with appropriate adjectives (such as are used by the children in their everyday English conversation). Plurals as well as singulars may be given. Every word should be written down on the board, that it may be seen as well as heard. From time to time, by way of revision, the pupils should be asked to spend twenty minutes in writing on their slates all the words they can remember. In doing this, they would naturally look about them to see the *things* which they were to name in French. This, too, is a pleasant exercise. The completion of this part of the course (indeed, the whole course itself) consists of object-lessons, just as these are given in English in the infant school. Compare Rules for Infant school teaching (Lecture III.).

Rule 4. As soon as practicable (perhaps from the first), give *est* and *sont* and *a* or *ont*, and make short sentences with the help of these words. Where simple sentences are possible, compound sentences, which are only simple sentences connected, are also easy. Thus by means of the sentence, the association, primarily one of things seen with the symbol, becomes an association of rational connection in a sentence.

Now may be introduced *de* and *du*, *de la* and *des*, and the sentence-making may be slightly extended. The conversational expressions of ordinary child conversation, almost always idiomatic, should be introduced.

I should not think it worth while to do more until English grammar is sufficiently well known. Much, however, depends on the age of the pupils and the skill of the master, as well as the time at his disposal.

Thus we give the pupil raw material; we exercise his ear and his tongue and pen from the first—essential in a modern tongue, in which our ultimate object is speaking and writing, and not merely the language of literature.

The one expression which is the key to the work of this stage is *Object-lesson*, and the blackboard will be in continual request. However easily a man may translate from a foreign tongue, he never feels that he has a firm hold of it unless his knowledge rests on the familiar, ordinary, and colloquial.

Rule 5. *Present to Sense.* The ear and eye (by the help of the blackboard) are brought into use in connection with every new word and sentence. The muscular sense is brought into activity in slate-writing, and in requiring the distinct vocalisation of the words and sentences by all the class simultaneously and (as far as possible) individually.

All this oral and blackboard instruction may be going on during the half-year preceding the use of a book.

Rule 5, and *Step after Step.* In the twelfth year, the learning of the Accidence has to be begun. This is essential to sound grammatical progress. It is best done by means of the blackboard and wall-sheets—nothing being introduced but what is regular.

By bringing in the law of the association of contrast and similarity, the learning of the inflexions of nouns, pronouns, and verbs may be made interesting and lively if the blackboard is first used, and the forms built up on it by the pupil under the master's guidance. When the pronouns and verbs are known, not a day should pass without saying some of them over as a kind of rote-exercise, until they can be said as quickly as the pupils can speak.

Extended object-lessons will now include names of ordinary acts familiar to the pupil—"speak" "do," "run," "think," etc., made into simple sentences.

An easy reading-book, beginning with a few simple

sentences on matters of everyday experience, may be introduced about the same time as the Accidence is begun. The material of the book should pass *rapidly* from simple sentences to very easy stories, and, ere long, to such conversations as *children might be supposed to carry on with each other*. The elementary books used in French primary schools seem to me to be at this stage the best reading books.

The use of the book is now and henceforth a central part of the instruction; but oral practice is always essential in learning a living language. In using the book, Rules 9, 10, and 11 ("Exactness and thoroughness," the "teaching of the salient and easy first," and persistent "turning to use," etc.) have all to be applied as in the case of Latin. The book is the centre round which the instruction turns, but it is yet *subordinate to the living oral instruction*.

The lesson having been read, the teacher—the pupils having their books shut—*speaks* the lesson clause by clause, and has it translated a second and third time in this way.

Meanwhile, yesterday's lesson has been handed in, having been written as a home exercise, and the teacher proceeds to read aloud the English of it, and call for its retroversion into French. This having been done orally, the pupils are sent to their seats to write out the French, the English being put on the board. The best scholar can then read aloud to the others from the book, while the others correct their exercises, the master glancing at a few as a check. The object is to get the book into the memory as living material which the children can use.

If there is time, the master now turns the narrative lesson into a subject of conversation. If the lesson be a dialogue, he takes one part while his pupils take the other. The pupils also carry on the dialogue with one another. In a living language there should be numerous dialogue lessons, until they pass into sustained conversations extracted from recognised books for the young. There are many such in French. Short dramatic pieces should be treated in the same way.

The reading books will gradually increase in difficulty; and alongside the thorough "lessoning" of one book there should always be found the rapid cursive reading of another book given out in the school and not taken home.

As to grammar and parsing: the rules common to English and French are brought into play at once. *Gradually*, the differences of the two languages are pointed out as they reveal themselves in the reading-book. These are illustrated on the board, and transferred by the children to a note-book as a home-lesson.

Rule 13 (*Associate Teachings*). Vocables are from the first associated with things seen. Thereafter with one another in sentences. The sentence must always be the unit, not a word by itself. Isolated lists of words and phrases learned by heart are of little use. The new is associated also with the old by comparing the new form with that already known.

In schools where Latin is taught, associate the Latin, French, and English forms of the same word, pointing out the differences of signification as well as of form.

It will be noticed that, if the above course be followed, every lesson is a lesson in composition, and that the whole atmosphere of the schoolroom is a French atmosphere. Formal composition exercises to be written at home, or in school, in the form of simple narrative,—the re-telling of a French story in such language as the pupil can command,—and the writing of letters, will, of course, have their due place; as also the learning by heart of simple French poetry. All this, just as it is done in the good teaching of the native tongue.

Bearing in mind the practical end of our teaching, we should let no day pass, after the first year, without *reading aloud* an "unseen," and calling for its oral translation into English.

It is assumed that as soon as possible the teacher asks questions in French, and takes for answer, not a yes, or no, or any one word, but a complete sentence.

I omit much, but the reader can easily further apply the suggestions under the head of English and Latin to French.

In this way a boy who is fourteen complete should have attained a good knowledge of French grammar, a satisfactory acquaintance with ordinary idioms, facility in reading at sight ordinary narrative in such French as that of Charles XII. and Télémaque,[1] a power of taking a part in *simple* French conversation, and of writing a simple letter in French.

To say more than I have said would be to sketch a series of lessons in French extending over three or four years, which the teacher might use in a mechanical spirit. The result would be failure. Schoolmasters, as I have elsewhere said, have to study Education in its end, its processes, principles, and methods; and then leave themselves free to think out detail in their general instruction-plan and in their daily teaching. This independence and vitality in the teacher are necessary to his success. Indeed, I ought almost to apologise for illustrating the application of the rules of method to French, as I have partially done.

To the study of French beyond the age of fourteen, Rules 14 and 15 for Latin are applicable in the strictest sense.

Conclusion.

My object in this course of lectures has been to demonstrate that Language must always be the governing subject in all education worthy of the name. It is the essential condition of growth. It provides a vehicle, ever growing with the growth of mind, for the expression of the inner life, without

[1] I name these simply for illustration.

which expression the deeper emotions and the spiritual suggestions of our complex nature are like the clouds on a windy day, ever changing their fleeting forms, and finally vanishing altogether. Only when shaped into words do these feelings and emotions get for themselves a body, and become to us a permanent possession. They then react upon our lives, and are the steps to higher things. By the assimilation of the language of others, mind is fed, and it is feeding that makes the evolution of mind in the young possible. Again, language as a real and concrete subject not only feeds, but, if it is understood, it *trains:* it trains the processes of intelligence without strain or effort, and whether a boy will or not. Further, I have endeavoured to point out the distinction between training and discipline, with a view to your seeing that, while the study of language, as vehicle of thought and feeling, trains, with grammar, it disciplines; thus its claims as an educational instrument become almost irresistible.

But not only does language feed, train, and discipline: it also at all stages, if properly taught, cultivates in us the beautiful and ideal through the forms of literature—as compared with which all other forms of art are of secondary and only ancillary importance. It is quite possible to teach literature, though it may be undesirable to examine on it. An external examination with its percentages, though, in most subjects, inevitable in these days, should not, I think, be allowed to degrade those more delicate instruments of school education which have to do with the ideal in any form, whether it be literature or religion. It is death to them. And yet, at the *university* stage there is material enough for examination in the subject of English: (1) grammar; (2) philology and word-history; (3) literary history; (4) explanation and criticism of a passage; (5) essay writing.

In speaking of the Method which is to be followed in teaching language if it is to be an educational instrument, I have given you rules, but I have not sought to dwell on these unduly. Enough has been done, however, to show how the teacher may elaborate rules for himself, and so work from within. Let him realise fully, and by much thought, the aim, the purpose, the idea of his daily work. Let him understand that he is using language in its various aspects in order to enrich and form, as well as to inform, the minds committed to him, and he will quickly find a method of procedure which may or may not embrace all the rules of Method which another may advocate, but which, though occasionally erring, will yet be better than a method imposed on him from without, because it will be a living, and not a mechanical, method. "The transmission of life from the living through the living to the living is the highest definition of education."[1] Method is a good servant but a bad master. In a teacher, however, as

[1] Thring, p. 27.

in men of every other occupation and profession, a man's originality is of little worth until he has first learned all that can be taught him; but when he has once learned this, let him then live his own professional life freely, for "it is the letter that killeth, but the spirit giveth life."

My purpose in these lectures, I need hardly say, has not been to depreciate science-teaching. On the contrary, there ought to be found in every school a graduated and organised system of realistic teaching from the infant-school to the gates of the university — the method of the object-lesson being in this department the key to all science method. We do not need to be afraid of as much encyclopædism as will place an educated youth in a rational attitude to nature. What God has thought it worth His while to make, is probably worthy of man's attention without derogating from his dignity, or insinuating an insult to Greek. Still, the centre round which all education of a man must revolve is, in my opinion, a humanistic centre, and I have, therefore, in these lectures ventured to re-state the case for Language, and say a word for Words.

Many things which I have suggested may seem small and trivial to some masters, but Quintilian says that the man to whom anything in education seems small is not a good teacher: in truth, are not the very greatest things made out of a large number of small ones, by which alone they become possible, just as the physical universe is made up of atoms? And what we educators aim at is a very big thing in its result, for "in very deed, in the end," as excellent Ascham simply says, "the good or ill bringing up of children doth as much serve to the good or ill service of God, our Prince, and our whole country, as any one thing doth beside."

SUPPLEMENT.

SUPPLEMENT.

Remarks on School-Instruction in the Classical Languages —especially Latin—as compared with Instruction in SCIENCE.[1]

IN considering this question, it is necessary to clear away from the field of discussion all illusory imaginations as to the larger proportion of boys who would benefit by a secondary-school system based solely on scientific training, as compared with the number which might benefit by the discipline afforded through the classical tongues if good methods were employed. Severe and sustained intellectual work, having knowledge or other mental purposes exclusively in view, is naturally distasteful to the great majority of boys. We must not draw too large an inference from the inquisitiveness and love of knowledge which characterise childhood. The recipient stage of a child's life should be gently and wisely dealt with, and this it is the function of the primary school to do. But in the middle school, receptivity has given place in the boy

---

[1] I venture to reprint this essay here because of its relevancy to the subject of this book, and because the volume in which it appeared is out of print, and will never be republished.

to force, which seeks not to accept impressions, but rather to make them. To break in upon the spontaneous and healthy expression of this fresh boyish energy with Latin prose composition, or classifications of birds and beasts, or chemical equations, is, even in the most favourable circumstances, to traverse the natural and genial current of young life, and to call for a painful and self-sacrificing exertion of will. Most boys will be found to make this exertion, when they do make it, not from love of the work itself, but from emulation, or from the moral considerations of respect for authority, of personal attachment, or a sense of duty. Of this we may be sure, that when inborn stupidity and rampant boyism have claimed their own, the residue of real intellectual workers, where there is no external motive to intellectual exertion, will always be found numerically disappointing. Nor will the substitution of pneumatics, physiology, and chemistry, for Latin and Greek, draw out a larger amount of talent than these do, or show better on the reckoning-day, when stock is taken of the quantity and quality of available knowledge and discipline really acquired. That by means of better books and of methods based on a knowledge of human nature, a much larger proportion of boys might be drawn within the circle of school-work, is undeniable; but this points to the improvement of existing practice, not to the subversion of the existing system of studies.

There are, it seems to us, only two valid objections to the prevalent practice of our public schools—(1)

The almost entire exclusion from these schools of elementary physics, history, and social economy, which, if properly taught, can be made attractive as well as instructive, promoting rather than retarding the magistral classical and mathematical studies. (2) The non-provision of a course of study for those pupils who do not contemplate an university career, and whose intellects, though repelled by linguistic subjects, might possibly be reached by those consecutive and methodical accounts of the external world which we call Science. If the study of Latin and Greek, as the leading subjects of middle-school work, renders once for all inevitable the total exclusion of all instruction regarding external nature, national history, literature, and economic science, the cause of the classicists is, by the admission of this necessity, fatally weakened. As a matter of fact, however, there is no difficulty in prosecuting the study of at least one ancient language, concurrently with those subjects which every educated man may be reasonably expected to know in their elementary principles and general purport. This amount of (so-called) *realistic* scientific knowledge is easy of attainment in secondary schools, and as imperative as it is easy. Such subjects as natural history are probably best treated by what might be called the recreative method, *i.e.* recreation with a plan in it.

It is only after we have assumed *a certain amount* of realistic instruction to be given in public secondary schools to all the pupils, and a separate educational provision for those who are by nature disqualified for linguistic discipline, that we properly approach the question of Language *versus* Science as an educative instrument; and the question then becomes this: Is physical science, as such, or are the classical tongues, when taught with average ability (for it is only on a mediocre teaching capacity that we ever can safely rely in estimating the value of subjects of instruction), more promotive of the formation of a good intellectual habit?

To state the question of a classical *versus* a scientific education as a training in the knowledge of the lifeless signs of speech and their relations, *versus* a training in a knowledge of living Nature and its manifold operations, is to misrepresent the point at issue. In the university, and in the upper classes of the middle school, the dispute is *not* between the claims of formal and of real studies. Both studies present the realities of knowledge to the mind of the student—the one the realities of man's nature, the other the realities of physical nature. Again, both Latin and physical science exercise and discipline the formal powers of intellect, and both admit the student to an unconscious knowledge of the operation and the laws of intelligence. But that the purely formal discipline of language (where we happen to have a highly developed language to work with) is more delicate and subtle, more deep and thorough, than that of physics, is, we think, justly to be maintained.

Apart from formal discipline, the superiority claimed for classical training over scientific consists in this, that in the former we have the generalisations of the wisest men on human life and human duty expressed in the most artistic forms; in the latter we have only generalisations on the facts and sequences of the visible world. The realities of moral experience, embodied in forms historical and dramatic, as these are impressed on the acquiring mind by the very effort applied in deciphering a difficult language, are of more value, both in themselves and as giving solidity and permanent power to the mental fabric, than a knowledge of the phenomena of heat and electricity. These moral generalisations of the wise are, in truth, an unsystematic philosophy of human nature, furnishing the learner not only with the experience of the past, but with instruction in the motives and purposes of life.

To become acquainted with the genius of the past through the medium of translation, or when transfused through modern literatures, is to sacrifice the benefits which we derive from the study of thought which has been produced in circumstances not only different from, but even in some respects antagonistic to, our own. It is to sacrifice also the artistic form in which these thoughts are clothed—forms which are the most perfect in literature, and which the structure of the ancient languages forces even upon the negligent student. The peculiar value of the æsthetics of the intellect and of morality, as distinguished from the æsthetics of feeling and emotion, in promoting the discipline and cultivation of mind, and above all of the opening mind of youth, has not been (so far as I know) adverted to by writers on education, though it must have been experienced by all who have had the benefits of a classical training. It is not simply an æsthetic, but also an intellectual and moral cultivation, which flows from close contact with ideal and artistic forms of utterance.

Such results in the growth of mind are, it is true, neither ponderable nor commensurable quantities, but they assuredly tend to produce a *quality* of mind rarely to be attained in any other way, save by men of native genius. Richter has well said, and probably without much exaggeration—" The present ranks of humanity would sink irrecoverably if youth did not take its way through the silent temple of the mighty past into the busy market-place of after-life."

But turning aside from classical education as a whole, let us confine ourselves to Language in general as an educational instrument: and let us consider the contending claims of language and science closely in their relation to the growth of intelligence.

As an intellectual discipline, language makes good its claim to preference on the following among other grounds :—

1. Words stand for things real or notional. Now it is only in so far as words denote the objects of external perception that a training based on science can be said to have advantage over linguistic training.

Even in this case, however, language is defined for the pupil only within the narrow limits of the department, or fragment of departments, which it is possible within a given time to teach; whereas linguistic training, by teaching the value of words, *as such*, to whatever department of human knowledge they may belong, educates the intellect to precision in the use of them generally. So true is this, that men trained only in a special department of science, and whose education is limited by it, fail to use the language even of their own department with that accuracy and consistency of signification which would alone satisfy a mind trained on language or philosophy. In the only sense, then, in which physical science, to *the extent to which it can be taught to boys*, can affect to do the work of linguistic training, it does not succeed. Even if it succeeded, how small the ground it would cover! The language of a single department of science or fragments of a few sciences, which, moreover, in so far as they are fragmentary, fail to yield true discipline, would represent the whole range of the vocabulary taught. All those words which are daily in our mouths as denoting the realities which are constantly influencing our lives in all social and moral relations, would be left outside the range of the scientific teaching. It would be superfluous here to dwell either on the pre-eminent importance of this aspect of man's daily existence, or on the immense value of a right understanding of words, and a wise use of them. Every successive inquirer into human nature has descanted on the error, misunderstanding, and consequent misery into which an abuse of words is constantly betraying mankind. It seems to me that if a linguistic training had no other result than to teach us that words were our servants and not our masters, and that we must question, define, weigh, and estimate them, it would require little other defence of its claim to the traditionary prominence in the secondary school which it happily inherits.

2. When we pass from the consideration of the discipline of language in teaching us the exact use of single terms, to the employment of these in the expression of our thoughts under the necessary operation of mental laws, we find in language a just, though imperfect, reflection of intellectual processes. In this view the study of language is the informal study of the laws of thought. We may assume that few will be prepared to require from boys that reflective grasp of intellectual laws, that effort after a conscious realisation of abstract processes, which is implied in any study of logic or psychology worthy of the name. At the same time, all will recognise the paramount importance of exercising the formal powers of mind, and, by a careful method, giving practice in the art, while avoiding the scientific terminology and formulæ of logic. Now it is precisely in this relation that the distinctive characteristic of language-training reveals itself. For language being the body of thought, the student of it is studying concrete mind. While dealing with objective things—with vocables, which are

audible and visible, and which, therefore, do not evade his grasp — he is at the same time unconsciously tracing the operations of intellect in others, and learning the right use of his own faculties; in other words, he is a student of logic, in the widest sense of that term, without being aware of it.

What I have said applies to Language in general, including the *vernacular* language above all. But the vernacular cannot be thoroughly known without the aid of another, and, above all, an ancient tongue; and for English-speaking people that tongue *must be Latin*. Let us look at this language as specially fitted to give the discipline to which I have referred above.

In the first place, the word-inflections in a Latin sentence lead the pupil to the clear perception of the concord and partial identity in thought of subject and attribute, whether the attributive appears as an adjective or a predicative verb. The distinct forms by which inflected languages indicate this mental concord must necessarily give the pupil a clearer notion of what a judgment and an affirmation really are. We do not here speak of the use which might be made of this part of linguistic discipline by a teacher who was himself conscious of the course of logic which his instructions in language were scarcely veiling, but of the *inevitable* discipline which the average boy receives from the average teacher. And it is not only in simple sentences that the pupil is thus exercised in the concord of thought as expressed in attribution, but he is also led by the help of the same mutual good understanding among the inflections to trace a connection between clauses, and to detect the fact that complete assertions, no less than individual words, may be attributive of each other. The tracing out and perception of this unity of the organism of thought as expressed in a series of related affirmations is a valuable intellectual exercise.

We pass over the clearness which must be given to the pupil's perception of time and of government (so-called) by the resembling, yet differing, terminations of verbs and nouns, to point out the training in syllogistic logic which he necessarily receives when he enters on the analysis of an involved complex sentence. The varying inflections of the words before him necessarily lead him to the discrimination of an assertion from its grounds, and of a conclusion from its causes, motives, or purposes. The forms set apart to denote these qualities of propositions compel his attention, detain it, and thus fix the distinctions in his mind. Again, those qualities of propositions which we express by the words hypothesis and probability, and even so fine a distinction as that between probability and possibility, are forced upon the understanding of the learner, however unconscious the teacher may be of the full meaning and value of the instrument he is using, and however ignorant the pupil may be of the logical generalisations of propositions and the names by which these generalisations are known. What higher discipline of intellect can be proposed for a boy whom we desire to discipline severely, but whose self-consciousness we do not yet wish to evoke, or to force into activity, than to lay before him a mass of words, apparently dead and disjointed signs, and to require that, from a steady consideration of these, the living organism of speech shall be built up—an organism into which all the formal elements of intellect run, and which calls for the discrimination, not only of the various relations in thought of the propositions before him, but of the precise force of many and various vocables, possessing, it may be, a wide and various connotation?

Nay, I would go further, and maintain that for the production of a purely scientific habit of intellect we shall best employ some years of boyhood in the study of an ancient synthetic language, and preferably of Latin. For such a study exercises the intelligence at once subtly and profoundly; it penetrates all the recesses of fallacy, and thereby habituates the mind to the search for exactness and truth—the highest of all qualifications for scientific investigation. While the study of an ancient tongue necessarily widens the conceptions, it also helps to elevate the intelligence above the dominion of words and phrases. This or that department of science is no longer the master of the scientific investigator, but his servant. It is seen in its true proportions as only a part of the general truth of life. Comprehension and grasp are thus given, and the man who after linguistic training becomes the thorough master of any one science, is truly a master of it, because he sees it in its true proportions and in its relations to the vast realm of knowledge. Setting aside men of genius, is not the man of one science, or even two, about the narrowest and most hopelessly barren of educated men?

The study of Latin, then, by giving comprehension of mind and power of intellect, is the best of all preparations for even the scientific man; and further, it gives greater acuteness of discrimination — a most important attribute of the highest scientific minds. In short, we may say that the formal study of language, and, above all, of Latin, is the most admirable of all exercises in the analysis and synthesis which constitute the whole method of science.

3. To the contention that the intellectual discipline of which we speak can be equally well obtained from subjects more immediately useful than an ancient tongue, such as the natural sciences, I would say:—

The instruction of boys, in all subjects in which the formal is, from the nature of the case, of primary importance, must be essentially dogmatic. It may be safely said that up-to the age of sixteen even a lucid statement of *principles* is received by all but a few boys as dogma: to suppose anything else is to deceive ourselves. Though they may be occasionally startled into the conscious perception of rational relations under the influence of a teacher of original mind, they do not, and cannot, in any adequate sense, realise the reasoning process by which scientific conclusions are reached. They are not trained in the method of science. Hence, while in the study of natural science, or any branch of it, they are doubtless taught not only facts, but classifications and laws, and causes in relation to their effects, these are not in the majority of cases elaborated by the pupil himself. The teaching of them, accordingly, is apt to degenerate into a statement of fact, and the learning of them into an act of memory.

It is to be at once conceded, that were pupils led by an intelligent and rarely-endowed master in an inquiry into nature, with a view to re-establish, for themselves, results already known, a training would by this means be given unequalled as a discipline; but such a method of instruction is on a large scale quite impracticable, and, even if practicable, it would be premature in its demands on a boy's powers. Those educationalists, who are not mere theorists, feel the necessity of finding an instrument which does not overstrain boys, and which can work fairly well in the hands of no very cunning workmen. Where natural science is that instrument, the method which looks so well in theory must degenerate in actual practice into the most ordinary and vulgar cram. Differences, generalisations, laws, and causes will not be truly apprehended *as such*, but will be arranged in the pupil's mind by virtue of association alone, however glibly they may be enunciated at call in their proper places and sequences. It is only the select few, even of those who fairly master the subject taught, that are fully conscious of the reasoning process involved, and do not simply trust to faithful memory and association. It is no doubt true that, a few years later, the boy who has been well taught in one or two departments of science may reflect on the results of that teaching, and in this way these results may fructify into a kind of retrospective discipline; the relation of cause and effect, differences, likenesses, and the elements and grounds of generalisations, may be then apprehended, and the intellectual ends of education be thus attained. But even the production of this winter-fruit assumes particularly good teaching, a good memory, and habits of mind which are naturally more than usually reflective.

In Latin, on the contrary, the intellectual processes of differentiation, generalisation, and reasoning are not only much more fully, delicately, and variously represented than in physics, but they have the signal advantage of not being offered to the learner as scientific *results* which are capable of being tabulated and acquired by the memory as so many co-ordinated facts. They have in every successive sentence to be sought out and brought to light *anew*, and this as the very condition of making a single progressive step. The boy's daily task is the constructing of a living organism out of a seemingly chaotic aggregation of dead symbols, and in the construction of this he brings into play all his intellectual faculties whether he will or not. The discipline is thus obtained independently of the teacher, and independently of the purpose of the pupil also.

Of no other instrument of discipline can this be said except geometry, and the kind of cultivation which it gives is of too narrow a kind to admit of its ever being more than the accessory of other educational instruments. The precision of the definitions in geometry, the necessity of constantly referring to them, and the purity of the exercise in syllogistic reasoning which it affords, are of great benefit to the young mind. But alone, and unsupported by the higher linguistic training, geometry would be an unsatisfactory and barren discipline. The subject-matter of the reasoning is confined within too narrow limits, and the landmarks of the ratiocinative process are too clearly defined, to admit of its ever affording by itself a liberal culture. Both the subject and the discipline which it gives, are too monotonous and inflexible.

In the study of Latin the boy either does the work before him or he does not: if he does it, he cannot, if he would, avoid obtaining the discipline which the work affords; whereas, in elementary science, the ready memory facilitates the acquisition of a semblance of knowledge which may pass muster, but which does not yield thorough discipline. We shall, perhaps, be told that boys can and do understand science teaching; but when we examine closely we find that the objectors do not really mean strict science at all, but only nature-knowledge, and this we have already said ought, as a matter of course, to have its place in every secondary school.

Accordingly, as in the training to a perception of

the force of vocables, so also in the disciplining of the formal and intellectual powers, there seem to be sufficient grounds for maintaining that science, *as it can be alone taught to boys between twelve and sixteen years of age*, is a feeble educative instrument as compared with a language like Latin.

The kind of discipline above claimed as the almost exclusive property of language in the field of secondary instruction, cannot be so surely obtained through the modern tongues, except in those cases (on which it would be vain to calculate) in which the rare excellence and general philological cultivation of the master supplement the inherent defects of his instruments. It is the contrast of the Latin tongue to our native mode of casting thought, no less than its own perfection of structure, that makes it so valuable as a discipline. The conspicuous devices, moreover, whereby grammatical, and therefore thought, relations are indicated, reveal, even to the careless pupil of the most ordinary teacher, the logical structure of all language. The organism of thought is more completely exhibited, the relation of its elements is more delicately indicated, and the unity of the whole is more conspicuously made visible in a classical tongue than in any other.[1]

If nature-knowledge and mathematics and modern

---

[1] The larger literary and æsthetic arguments in favour of basing secondary education on the classical tongues are not here discussed. Our object has been simply to show the nature of the intellectual operations which language on the one hand, and science on the other, calls into play in boys between twelve and sixteen.

languages, including our own language, are all admitted to a place in our secondary schools, I grant that it is impossible to preserve to both Latin and Greek their present practical monopoly. The ship must be lightened or it will never reach its port. Greek, in short, must, to our loss, cease to be a necessary subject in secondary schools. It must be a special subject to be taken by those who choose. I do not believe in what are called "modern sides" in classical schools. Education at the secondary stage is an unity, as it is in the primary stage. It is only after sixteen or seventeen that the process of specialisation can be allowed to show itself. To exclude Latin, however, as well as Greek from the obligatory curriculum, would be an educational calamity. Being the storehouse of a large portion of our own tongue, it yields in quite a peculiar degree an exercise in the history and force of words. In studying Latin we are studying our native, if not strictly our mother, tongue, and it is impossible to acquire a command of modern English if we are ignorant of one of its sources. When we remember that Latin is the basis of the Romance languages, and smooths the way to an acquaintance with these, we add the consideration of utility to an already adequate ground of preference.

MORRISON AND GIBB, PRINTERS, EDINBURGH.

www.ingramcontent.com/pod-product-compliance
Lightning Source LLC
Chambersburg PA
CBHW032059230426
43662CB00035B/741